Don't Wait Until You Graduate II

Don't Wait Until You Graduate II

*Jump-Start Your Career in Today's Volatile Economy
While Still in School*

Keith F. Luscher

New Horizon Press
Far Hills, New Jersey

Copyright © 2003 by Keith F. Luscher

All rights reserved. No portion of this book may be reproduced
or transmitted in any form whatsoever, including electronic,
mechanical or any information storage or retrieval system, except
as may be expressly permitted in the 1976 Copyright Act or in
writing from the publisher. Requests for permission should be
addressed to:

New Horizon Press
P.O. Box 669
Far Hills, NJ 07931

Keith F. Luscher
    Don't Wait Until You Graduate II: Jump-Start Your Career in Today's
    Volatile Economy While Still in School

Cover Design: Mike Stromberg/The Great American Art Company
Interior Design: Susan M. Sanderson

Library of Congress Control Number: 2003100078

ISBN: 0-88282-228-4
New Horizon Press

Manufactured in the U.S.A.

2007   2006   2005   2004   2003   /   5   4   3   2   1

Dedication

For Leanne, Jacob, Camille, Simon and Isabelle

Table of Contents

Acknowledgements   ix

Introduction   Why You Need This Book   xi

Chapter 1   Life After Graduation—Why You Must Not Wait   1

Chapter 2   Breaking Down the Barriers   7

Chapter 3   The First Giant Leap…Volunteer!   15

Chapter 4   Where to Find Service Opportunities   29

Chapter 5   The Two Faces of Networking   43

Chapter 6   Start Building Your Network   63

Chapter 7   Small Companies, Big Opportunities   79

Chapter 8   Short-term Work, Long-term Benefits: Internships and Summer Employment   95

Chapter 9   Service Learning: Education Through Experience   115

Chapter 10   Hire Yourself! Start Your Own Business   125

Chapter 11   Getting Noticed: An Idea Jogger to Help You Stand Out   141

Conclusion   What Goes Around, Comes Around   159

Appendix I   Organizations that Need Your Help   165

Appendix II   Campus and Community Resources   197

Appendix III   Media Resources   201

Appendix IV   Send Me Your Questions!   215

Notes   217

Acknowledgments

I would like to acknowledge all those who were of assistance, either directly or indirectly, in the writing, editing or publication of this book:

Rita Cohen
David Mustine
Kendra Frank
Roger Beckett
Thomas P. Luscher
Gayle Hillecke
Pam Boylan
Denise Pittenger
Herb Lape
Martha Rosenson
James O. Belcher
Karen Mahaffey
Leanne R. Luscher
Gerald Maloney
Steve Mariotti

Introduction

Why You Need This Book

The decade of the nineties and our transition into the new century has been an economic roller coaster. Within just a few years, we have witnessed how perception can fool reality. Investors pumped billions of dollars in venture capital into Internet startups, many of which had no business opening their doors. Then, as the "gold revealed itself as pyrite," companies which had employed tens of thousands at almost unheard-of salaries fell one by one. Not long after, America suffered the tragedy of thousands dying in the terrorist attack on the World Trade Center and Pentagon.

Both the economic boom and the illusion that the United States was safe from the catastrophes of terrorism were destroyed.

A changing world, and in some cases a scary one. As a student sitting on the sidelines, you witnessed these changes and the ongoing reports on the fluctuating state of the economy. Up, down, up, down. In the back of your mind (or perhaps in the front), you may be asking yourself: What can I possibly do now while I'm still in college to help ensure that my giant educational investment will pay off?

How will all this affect me? What can I do to take control?

First of all, let's get one thing straight. This is not a book about *job hunting*. Job hunting is a process, which includes searching for openings, sending out resumes and cover letters and interviewing. The goal of the process is to get someone else to be impressed enough with you that they will offer you a job.

This process, along with our world economy, has changed dramatically over the last several years. Yes, technology has made it easier for you to circulate your resume. But I have a tip for you: *it's made it easier for everyone else too!* Today, companies receive twenty to fifty times more resumes than in the past and there are less job openings. Sources at *Staffing Industry* magazine indicate as many as thirty million resumes are circulated in the United States *each month!* And, according to the Wall Street Journal, almost two million jobs were eliminated between March 2001 and January 2003.

Executive recruiters will be the first ones to tell you that your resume is not going to get you the job. *You are.* People will employ you based not on your resume, but your character, your work ethic, and your talents. How can you convey all of that in a single-page letter or a twenty-minute interview? The truth is, you can't.

"Jump-starting" your career is not about searching for your first job. It's about doing what you can *before your job hunt begins:* investing your time while still in school to build upon three personal characteristics— your integrity, your skills and your relationships. Begin focusing on these traits, and your career will have begun before you know it. This principle is true in good economic times, as well as bad.

This book will show you how to do it.

Let's first quickly review the differences between the terms "job" and "career."

A job, in our context, is defined in Webster's dictionary as "something that has to be done; a specific duty, role or function." A suggested synonym is the word "task."

A career, on the other hand, is defined as "a pursuit of consecutive progressive achievement—a profession for which one trains and is undertaken as a permanent calling."

Most college students tend to define the beginning of their careers in terms of when they land their first jobs. The problem is they have it backwards. Your career does not begin with your first day on a job. Your career begins the moment you start using your mind and talents to implement your future and start to positively influence the lives of those around you.

Now More than Ever...

As you know by now, this message is more urgent today than ever before. You are paying big bucks for a college degree. At one time, a diploma was considered a virtual meal ticket, but not anymore.

Before I go much further and get myself into trouble, I first want to remind you that you must still complete your educational goals. I have no doubt that many students who adopt these principles will actually find jobs before graduation. A few of them might drop out of school, never to earn their degrees (I know some who have). This is a grave mistake of shortsightedness.

Just remember: you must not wait until you graduate—but you must graduate.

The Catch-22 Fallacy

When I was in college, I heard the same old complaint all the time (and sometimes muttered it myself): I can't get experience without a job, and I can't get a job without experience!

This statement is false 98 percent of the time. The fact is you can get experience without a job, and you can get a job without experience. Trust me. It happens, and it's simpler than you think.

Take the Fear Out of the Future

I know what many of you are thinking. Through our economic ups and downs, you can't stop noticing bleak headlines concerning the age of specialization, company downsizing, job layoffs and the shrinking need for manpower in many areas. Perhaps it was true when you were a freshman that graduating seniors had their pick of where to work. Today, you may be hoping just for a single offer when your time comes.

The problem with this attitude is that it takes control out of your hands and places it in the hands of fate:

- You hope the economy will not just be good, but great.

- You hope that your grades and limited experience will be good enough.
- You hope you pick the right major.
- You hope a good job will be waiting for you when you graduate.

Until then, you feel that all you can do is study—and hope.

That's a fearful attitude. It's a gambling attitude. If you are afraid of the future—and most of us are, to a certain extent—then, you must step into it, today.

What's Missing in the Job-Hunt Equation: *Jobs versus Needs*

So much of the information today on jobs and careers focuses on the "marketing" side of it. In job-hunting, this means resumes, cover letters, interview skills, dressing for success and so on.

Why do we place such a heavy weight on these things? Why do we focus on the presentation rather than the product?

Presentation is important—there is no doubt about that. However, you run into a problem when you place more emphasis on the presentation than on what you are presenting.

In this book, we will focus on the latter: you. You are the product. Your education is the development of that product. What you must realize is that there is much more you can and must do to jump-start your career right now, before you graduate (and this doesn't mean waiting until your senior year, either) rather than after commencement ceremonies. This is true, even if you are a freshman with no idea of what you want to do with your life.

Perhaps what is missing most in the job-hunt equation is the fact that, by focusing too much on a job, *you may miss the need.* In other words, a person or entity may not have a job to offer you, but they may have a need that you can fill.

To take advantage of this, begin your career in college by searching for needs. This includes community needs, business needs and needs that exist everywhere.

Diffuse the Power of the Resume!

Even with the rapid influence of technology, today's job-hunting mentality gives too much power to the resume and other familiar job-hunting routines. This book will show you how to develop and display the skills, work ethic and reputation that will *precede* such introductory devices. It will show you how to build relationships with others who can open many doors to opportunity.

By doing this, you will reduce the resume, cover letter, and even the job interview to what they should be: mere formalities.

In this book you will also learn how to:

- Discover your own professional strengths and weaknesses.
- Determine what fields you really enjoy and are inclined towards if you are undecided.
- Understand your role in today's employer-employee relationship.
- Appreciate the value of your abilities and how they affect other people's lives.
- Find out the ten lifelong benefits of volunteer service and how to apply them.
- Seek and contact dozens, if not hundreds, of people who can put you to work today.
- Gain the benefits of building relationships over building contacts, and how to do both.
- Uncover the truth behind the biggest myth in networking: "It's who you know."
- Discover a secret for connecting with people in high places.
- Connect with people who will hire you, before you officially start looking for a job.
- Search for employers' needs before looking for employment.
- Begin thinking of yourself as a product and strategize how to market that product.

  ...and much, much more.

The Secret to Luck

It hasn't been too long since I was in your shoes. But when I (finally!) graduated from college with a degree in journalism, I had already been working as a communications manager for a medium-sized company ($75 million) for almost two years. While many of my fellow graduates were looking to become "temporary" waiters or bank tellers, I was fortunate to be earning an above-average salary and had already accumulated a considerable amount of experience. You might say that I lucked out.

But was it luck? Well, that depends upon how you define the word. The late Earl Nightingale[1] said that luck occurs "when preparedness meets opportunity. And opportunity is there all the time."

This may be what happened in my case. When I was hired, it was not in response to an advertisement. I did not go through the conventional interview process competing with hundreds or even dozens of other applicants. I didn't even have a resume.

Here's how it happened:

I was a junior in the Ohio State Journalism School. I had transferred there after studying art and design for over two years at another college, and I wanted to finish my degree in journalism.

At that time, desktop publishing was just emerging as a new tool of communications. As many of you may know, this is the process of using desktop computer technology for the typesetting, layout and production of printed materials. It was an industry which demanded the skills of both a writer and designer. These two skills, I had.

Was I excited! I had only one problem: I knew nothing about computers, let alone desktop publishing.

The only exposure I had to computers at that time was in a 100-level computer course required at school. The course work was very superficial; it concerned teaching methods, but not how to apply or benefit from them. Think of it as learning to drive a car, but not knowing how to choose or reach a destination.

The other major problem was mine: my only goal at that time was to get passing grades in the computer class.

So there I was. Eager to learn desktop publishing, I made a few trips to the university computer laboratory to "experiment" with the systems there. It was then that I realized something about myself: "experimenting" does not usually teach me much. I learn best by deciding upon a specific objective and striving for it.

Then one day, I was speaking to a teaching assistant in the J-school about desktop publishing, and she gave me the name and telephone number of someone who had contacted the school looking for some outside help. This man was the division president of a local building products supplier. It turned out that his company had purchased a desktop publishing system to improve their huge, 500-page catalog and marketing communications. The system was up and running, but he had no one to operate it.

At the time, I had very limited experience (much less than I probably let on). But I was prepared to go in and learn, even offering to work the first week or two for free (they still insisted on paying me). At that time, being a college student, needing a part-time job, and with really nothing to lose, I saw it as a win-win situation.

To my surprise, I knew enough to get started and eventually trained myself to near-expert level in just a few months. I was also producing tangible results with which the boss was pleased from my first day on the job.

Within a few short months, the part-time job became full-time and I found myself in the uncommon position of having created my own employment.

Was it luck? According to Earl Nightingale's definition, it surely was. I was prepared to take a risk. And when the opportunity presented itself, I had the clairvoyance to see and exploit it.

I wasn't the most qualified person to fill that position at the time; that is certain. There was only one reason that I was hired: the president of the company had a need, and I was the only person within the sound of his voice who could fill it.

Many college students today need to find the right perspective when it comes to career development. So often we hear the expressions, "I need a job" or "Give me a job." This connotes being given something.

If that's the way you envision it, open the newspaper. You aren't the only one who wants or needs a job. For every available position there are hundreds of qualified applicants. Many are more qualified than you. Many will work for less money. It is a buyer's market out there and that is not likely to change significantly in your favor during the course of your career.

What Do You Have to Offer?

You must learn how to seek out and recognize an opportunity to help someone else and be prepared to utilize it.

You must look for needs.

You must also realize that starting a career is most often a gradual process. So many job-hunt guides and manuals present a "road map" approach, promising results within a given period of time if you follow their specific steps.

I wish it were that easy. The reality is that there is no clear-cut path to a fulfilling career, or the job (or business) of your dreams. Success really occurs when you consistently implement a multitude of strategies, and sooner or later, with persistence and patience, something good results.

Half the strategy, though, is recognizing that "something" when it presents itself. It doesn't necessarily come in the form of a job offer or even an interview.

The other flaw in those books that promise so much is that they forget to mention that your success in the job market depends upon other people's decisions.

You've heard the expression, "Sell yourself!" That's true. But so often there is a misguided overemphasis upon grades and even skills. The important question is not what you can do, but how can you benefit someone else?

This book will help you explore the answers to these questions and help *you plant the seeds* for your career before you graduate.

Not Qualified? Qualify Yourself!

By adopting these few simple attitudes and strategies, you can develop a firm basis by which you can qualify yourself to be hired. We will discuss some key strategies for doing this. Many of them involve volunteerism and building relationships. Such enterprises will develop and refine the more important skills employers seek out, some of which include communication, initiative and the ability to relate to and work with other people.[2]

You will also learn how an attitude of service will build a strong character and work ethic, which will be recognized and appreciated by others.

Begin to contemplate your career goals (if you have not done this yet, start now) in terms of how you can benefit other people. After all, that's the true nature of capitalism: finding a need, filling it and accepting the earned rewards of doing so.

As you progress, while you may feel at times encouraged, and other times frustrated about the work world you are preparing to enter, it's my goal to help you understand the true meaning of service and the many rewards that it will bring. I'm not talking about service as in the military or government specifically. I am speaking about doing whatever you do, with an emphasis on improving people's lives, be they customers, clients, constituents or your next door neighbor.

A Special Request

After you learn and begin to apply these principles, I have one special request of you. Get in touch with me, either by letter, phone, or E-mail (see information in the back of the book) to let me know how you are progressing. Tell me how this book has helped you, and how it may be improved. I also want to hear about your success in jump-starting your career, so that I may tell your story to others in future editions of this book.

Don't forget to share your pitfalls too. Everyone has them! I will be happy to protect your anonymity if you so choose.

I also sincerely hope that you will learn one undisputable fact: *the world needs you.*

The question is, how will you respond?

I hope to share my strategies with you so that if the calling is within you to pursue a particular goal, you will know it. I also wish to share with you the proper resources so you can learn more on your own about beginning your career—not in the future, but now.

Life After Graduation—
Why You Must Not Wait

My dad doesn't envy me.

A retired corporate attorney, he spent his life working for fewer than five companies and pretty much viewed career progression from the old corporate perspective: you spend your first years finding your niche, and after a while you settle with one company, which, providing you work reliably, in turn will take care of you until you retire.

Of course, he knows it's different now. He's just relieved he's not playing by today's rules.[1] I know because he tells me that all the time.

Changing Times—Knowing Where You Stand

So where does that leave the rest of us? Most of our parents, regardless of their pursuit or education, grew up counting on eventually landing jobs or beginning professions in one place and remaining there for thirty to forty years. Today, that's no longer the story.

This mind-set came out of an era long past when American companies in the profit or non-profit areas could afford to promise near-lifetime security for their workers. The same promise was true for those who entered the professions, when becoming a doctor, lawyer, or teacher meant lifelong security. What an unrealistic expectation! Yet it was common back in the 1950s, when the United States, virtually the only industrial nation not ravished by World War II, was producing half of the world's goods and facing a time of glowing affluence. Those *abnormal* times in global competition[2] are hailed as an era of great economic prosperity for our country.

Unfortunately, that era also set an unrealistic standard that people began to expect. Both American business and government, in the wake of growing global competition and reduced revenues, became less able to meet that standard.

But global competition is not the only reason American companies adopt the strategy of *downsizing* both blue- and white-collar positions. Technological changes have changed the need for workers. American corporations have been eliminating more than two million jobs per year.[3] Many professions such as law, medicine and education are dealing with changing needs due to a shrinking or graying population, as well as an over-abundance of qualified practitioners.

Can we blame American business institutions or government? Personally, I don't think so, at least not entirely. After all, in the case of business, all exist to make a profit. That's why they hire employees. If there are no profits, there is no business, hence no jobs at all. And *fewer* jobs are better than *no* jobs.

(**NOTE**: If you think these are the opinions of someone who has never stood in an unemployment line with a family to support, they are *not*. I have been there, and I'll discuss that experience later.)

Jobs Are Not an End. *They Are a Means.*

In today's society, we so often hear about the government embarking upon programs for "job creation" to improve our nation's standard of living. This attitude completely misses the point.

Our quality of life does not get better with more *jobs* being created. A higher standard of living can only be accomplished when *problems are solved or needs are filled* through projects and achievements of individuals, groups, institutions or businesses.

Building a road to nowhere merely to keep paid workers occupied is ridiculous. The questions to ask are, "Where should that road go?" or "Do we need a road at all? If not a road, just what *do* we need?"

We should decide on our needs first and look at jobs, by which we *employ* our nation's human resources, as a means to fulfilling those needs.

That is why jobs are not an end. *They are a means.*

Likewise, businesses exist to make money by selling a product or service and meeting community needs. Jobs are simply by-products of this process.

Does that mean jobs are less important than profits? On an over-all economic scale, of course not. One cannot exist without the other. In order for a business to have sales, it needs customers with the income to spend. Fewer people with jobs means fewer customers, so it really is a self-supportive cycle.

While I'm no expert in economics, I hope you have a general idea of where jobs stand in economics. Business managers, however, look at the bottom line—not how their decisions will affect the over-all economy. They "buy" employees the way most of us ought to shop: by seeking the most in a person at the lowest cost.

Roger & Me

Unfortunately, far too many people, either on a conscious or unconscious level, think that business exists solely to create jobs.

In his highly acclaimed documentary film, *Roger & Me*, writer-director Michael Moore profiles his hometown of Flint, Michigan, in the aftermath of a massive General Motors plant closing.

He begins with GM's history in Flint, illustrating how GM and Flint were "perfect partners" thirty years ago. General Motors was by far the single largest employer in the region, with about 30,000 employees.

This placed GM in the position to literally make or break Flint. Unfortunately, the company did both.

The theme (hence the title) of the film was Moore's quest to interview then-GM Chairman Roger Smith, to answer personally for the plant closing.

Now, I'm not defending General Motors for closing those plants and laying off thousands of people; but I can't simply put all the blame on the company for Flint's problems, either. Unfortunately, this is just what Moore appears to do.

In the film, a General Motors representative tells Moore that simply because of its history in Flint, GM does not owe a huge debt to the community. What he appears to mean is that it is not the company's obligation to provide cradle-to-grave security for every employee.

A response off-camera: "Why not?"

The truth is, no matter how dismaying or unfair it may seem, no company or person is under that kind of obligation.

It Is Nobody's Obligation to Employ You

There are three important lessons to be gained from the Flint experience. The first is *never put all your eggs in one basket*, which is a mistake many of us make. In other words, don't rely too much on one person or company or professional firm to be there for you. Always try to keep your options open. This is easier said than done, but it is important.

The second is, while Michael Moore and even *you* personally may believe otherwise, *no company, institution or organization is obligated to provide you or anyone else cradle-to-grave security*. I challenge you to find a single business owner or executive in this country who will argue with that statement.

Regardless of how you feel personally, what matters are the opinions of those who do the hiring. This thought may not be comforting, but it is reality.

The third lesson is that you must *assume responsibility for your own life*. Don't blame others for the problems today's generation is facing. Throughout American history, every generation has had its unique challenges, passed down from the generations before.

There are fewer jobs in many fields once thought of as passports to prestige, and a widening gap between the economic classes. But we have nothing to gain by pinning the blame on someone else or avoiding reality.

In all this, *we still have the freedom to choose*. Life will throw hurdles, and we may not always be able to control them. But, as Ross Perot says, "Those who are most successful are those who are prepared to handle the unexpected."

New Times, New Generations

Every generation has its challenges. My generation, called "Generation X," faced economic recession in the early nineties—the recession that prompted me to write the previous edition of this book. The job market we faced was so unfriendly that we sometimes wondered why the heck we had gone to school in the first place. Many of us headed back to our parents' homes to live after graduation—which didn't please us or our parents very much.

Eventually our country rebounded from that recession and entered a sustained period of economic growth unprecedented in its history. However, it now appears that those "long boom" years are over. Today's "Generation Y"—which includes anyone born between 1977 and 1994—is now facing the same kind of recession I saw in the early nineties. Younger workers who, not too long ago, hoped to share in the economic abundance of the dot-com and Internet start-up boom years saw those dreams crash and burn.

When the national jobless rate climbs, younger workers suffer disproportionally, often reaching jobless rates that are three times worse than the national average. Here's why:[4]

Lack of experience and skills. Younger workers are more at risk, because employers want skills and proven performance. For the members of Generation Y, this is the first real sense of vulnerability they will experience.

Cuts in the tech industry. High school and college-age students were disproportionately represented in the high-tech industry which was hit very hard by the economic downturn.

Job displacement. Climbing unemployment has increased competition for jobs, causing older workers with more experience to take the entry-level jobs typically filled by younger hires. Younger workers don't have the work experience to be protected in a downturn.

These economic fluctuations are a blow to younger people, who feel they're victims of bad timing (believe me, I know the feeling!). A survey in 2000 showed that 75 percent of college students thought they'd be millionaires someday.[5] Today, most college students would be happy to simply get a job.

Wait, There's Hope...

This book will guide you in the right direction for jump-starting your career. The concepts are relatively simple, but that doesn't mean they're always going to be easy to implement. What you must understand is that the road to finding a job, especially for a new graduate, can be very long and sometimes very discouraging.

This is especially true when new graduates take no preliminary steps during their college years. If they just go to class, wait tables or deliver pizzas and little else, where does that leave them when it's time to find "real" work and make some "real" money? These are the people who end up applying at the *front door* for work. They mass-mail resumes and cover letters. They call on new people not for the enthusiasm of becoming acquainted or working together on shared objectives, but because they *want* something: *a job*.

Don't make these same mistakes. Instead, realize that there are actions you can take now which can turn your luck around. If you use the steps and follow the strategies I have outlined in the following chapters, you can turn these negatives into positives.

For example, after reading the chapters about volunteering and interning, you will learn about ways to show today's managers—even the ones who have negative perceptions of young people—that you have exactly the skills, abilities and work ethic that they are looking for. After reading the chapter about networking, you will realize that, despite downsizing and changes in technology, there are many ways to use your network to find new job opportunities and to get and stay employed. And after you apply the techniques you learn throughout the book, and develop the skills which will make you—and therefore your future employer, a success—then what company won't want to hire you for life?

So keep reading. Even better, start thinking about what you *would like* to do. What is it about your chosen field that excites you the most? If you have not chosen a field, think about what subjects and areas excite you. Focus on making this process enjoyable and fulfilling. If you are still in school, it is likely that the pressure to get hired hasn't kicked in yet. That makes NOW the best time to get started.

Whatever you do, *don't wait until you graduate!* Read on. Take action now to make your future a success.

Breaking Down the Barriers

"School is weird. You don't feel very old, but you don't feel very young. But it is important to see yourself, no matter what your age, as someone who can contribute instead of someone who is just taking."
- Ashley Valentine-Derrer
Capital University
Music/Christian Education

When Ashley arrived as a freshman at Capital University, she wanted to pursue a career in vocal performance, and she got involved in various Columbus opera and choir groups. But during that year, Ashley and a friend also got involved in a Big Sister volunteer program through the college. This program changed her life.

"During my freshman year, after I started volunteering with Big Brothers/Big Sisters, it was then that I began to see myself more as someone who can make a difference, as opposed to someone just out of high school who just thought of myself."

Ashley's new views about herself and her place in the world made her realize that her career would take a different path than the one she had intended. She decided to get more involved with her community, so she volunteered as an intern in a Christian education program with a large, Methodist church. This proved to be Ashley's calling.

"Even though I later decided to move into Christian Education, I didn't change my major, which some people wondered about," Ashley recalls. "Music majors are among the top hired majors in big companies, because of the intense discipline required to succeed. So I stuck with it, and I still perform." Ashley also notes that, "It's important, especially in a liberal arts school, to study what you like. You can do whatever you want with a good solid liberal arts degree in almost any field."

Ashley considered going directly to seminary in the fall, until members of the congregation encouraged her to apply for the position of Director of Christian Education. "I found out that if you go into something that you really like, it shows in the quality of the results you produce. The people you are serving will work hard either to keep you or help you advance."

Ashley got the director position, and she was soon in charge of overseeing the church's entire education area. With the valuable assistance of lay leaders, she had numerous programs up and running, while also coordinating the senior high and middle school youth fellowships.

From these experiences, Ashley learned that volunteering and interning while still in school are some of the best ways to get advanced field experience, which can help in knowing the direction you really want to take your career.

Ashley completed her education at United Theological Seminary in Dayton, Ohio. She now serves as a minister. Her advice to other students: "School is weird. You don't feel very old, but you don't feel very young. But it is important to see yourself, no matter what your age, as someone who can contribute instead of someone who is just taking. You always have *something* to give, and if other people see that, they will be happy to teach you and help you learn and grow."

"Get working. Volunteer. Find a service or a great internship program. You can find them in surprising places—who would have thought of a church? Get people to know you. There are connections everywhere, and you will also get to know yourself better. You will find out what you like and don't like."

Change is Good

While Ashley was in college, she learned to see herself not just as an individual, but as a member of a larger community. By volunteering her time and contributing to that community, Ashley helped others—and she also helped herself. Ashley realized that although she still enjoyed singing, she no longer wanted to make that her career. Instead, her service opportunities allowed Ashley to recognize that serving her community through the ministry would best suit her talents. By breaking down her barriers and seeing herself in terms of the world around her, Ashley put herself on the right career path, and today she has a promising future ahead of her in a job that she enjoys.

Now I'd like to help you break down any barriers you might have, and start you off on your own path to a rewarding career.

Arguments (or Excuses) Against Jump-Starting Your Career

Much of what this book deals with is **change**. College students who finish school and enter the workforce are often overwhelmed by the changes working brings about in their lives, and they become uncertain about breaking new barriers. Some of you may feel that the principles in this book may not apply to you. However, there is no question about the benefit they can bring to your future. This is true regardless of where you want to take your career.

The principles of this book center around:
- Your integrity, work ethic and dedication to service
- Your relationships with other people and how they know you

"I don't have the time."

Many of you are probably working a part- or full-time job to get by and put yourself through school. When I was in school, I was always working at least one job to pay the rent. Add that to my classes, and my schedule seemed pretty packed.

Of course, I knew nothing about how valuable my time really was. Once I graduated, that time didn't get any cheaper.

How much is your time worth? Are you *investing* it?

You are if you're in school. You are not getting paid to attend school. But when you graduate, you will have an asset that no one will ever take away from you: a college degree. With it comes knowledge and perceived credibility. These things will help you attain a career that will hopefully support you and benefit other people for the rest of your life.

But you must do more than just take classes.

You have heard the phrase, "Time equals money." It is so true. *And now, your time can be obtained at a bargain price!* Recent Census Bureau Statistics reveal that, on average, individuals in the traditional post-college age group (twenty-two to twenty-five year olds) earn less than $25,000. Most of you will discover this when you land your first job—real or temporary.

So why should your employer be the only one to get a bargain? You should too.

Good basic money management balances the demands of today with the needs of tomorrow, suggesting that you always invest a portion of your income for the future, diverting the rest to pay today's bills. Well, the same philosophy applies to time.

In fact, as financially strapped as most of us are these days, it should be easier to do with time than with money.

Look at your schedule and decide how much of your time is, or can become, available. Even if it's only five hours a week—that's twenty hours a month.

After all, there are no strict time minimums or maximums to jump-starting your career. It is an ongoing process, with only a small set of guidelines. You are going to be taking simple steps that will produce great results over the long haul. At the risk of using a common analogy, you will be planting seeds that will produce a much larger crop. This will make you much better prepared as you begin your job search.

For those who still insist they have no time, that this is not important enough to them, I say this: stop reading. Take this book back to the store and get a refund. Better yet, give it to a friend, or donate it to the library.

Of course, I trust that since you are still reading, you feel you do have *some* time to invest. Then I urge you: *don't wait until you graduate!* Ask yourself what your life will be like the day after graduation if you don't start building relationships and making contacts and getting experience in communication and working with people.

This is what it comes down to: *make time* to invest in jump-starting your career, getting experience and being a friend to others just as you make time (either willingly or not) for the other things in your life that are important. Remember that time equals money. Invest it as such. This book will direct you to some great resources on how you can accomplish this.

"I don't know anybody."

You have heard the expression: "It's who you know." Later, you will learn the reality behind that statement.

Nevertheless, getting connected in an industrial, institutional or governmental position or profession is like eating an Oreo® cookie: there is no single way to do it. In fact, there are dozens if not hundreds of ways.

One thing is true though. It takes time. That's why you must start now. In fact, you've probably already started and don't know it. If you don't believe me, try this exercise, and you will be surprised at how many people you know.

Take one normal work week, and write down the names of everyone you meet or associate with on a consistent basis. Include teachers, counselors, your boss at your job, other workers, etc. Now add that to people you have known for a long time—neighbors and family friends from home and friends of your parents and siblings. Are you a member of a church or synagogue? Who do you know there?

By now, the list is getting pretty long. What's even better is that each of those people knows a whole list of others to whom you may eventually be introduced. I'm not going to try to teach you how to network here, or how to make the list longer. I just hope I've shot down that excuse.

One point that I will reiterate throughout this book: you must not concentrate on "networking" as it is commonly known. You do not necessarily want to collect the most names—you want to build relationships.

"I have no idea what I want to do!"
In chapter 3, which is about volunteering, one of the topics discussed is that there are countless opportunities to discover what kind of service you enjoy and at which you excel. You can also attain a greater awareness of your strengths and abilities. If you aren't sure about what you want to do, then that's even more reason to start working, get involved in your community, and build relationships.

The other point is this: what you actually *choose* makes little difference while you're in school. Most of your professional education takes place *after* you finish school. College preps you to *enter* the work force. It's up to you to keep afloat and to succeed. The habits here will not only open up more opportunities before and after you graduate, but will empower you to face the challenges you encounter throughout your career.

There is a select group of qualities we will talk about developing throughout the course of this book. This group includes things like communication skills, initiative, relationship-building and the demonstration of a positive work ethic. These are the things that employers look for *above all else*. These are the things you will learn to develop. It may also include unique accomplishments that no one will ever be able to take from you.

Adopting the strategies and attitudes described here is more important to your future career than having a chosen major.

"My field requires a degree first."
Obviously, a medical student cannot perform surgery or even prescribe drugs, and a law student cannot defend other people's legal rights in a courtroom. However, there are a myriad of opportunities available in these fields to give you experience and reinforce or contradict your goal. For example, a prospective doctor might obtain a weekend or part-time job driving an ambulance or working in a hospital or other medical institution. Prospective lawyers may intern or work part-time in a law firm or government setting doing legal research.

Service.
Working with others.
Setting goals and communicating them.
Listening to others.

Moreover, what is the essence of these and many other professions?

If you can't do these things effectively, then the highest test scores you get in school won't save you. These are the qualities employers look for much more than grades, yet they cannot be taught in the classroom.

But as you will find, regardless of your education level, there are people who need you and your skills. You will learn how to get in touch with them.

The attempt to push beyond Mach 1—"breaking the sound barrier"— set for October 14, 1947. Not being an engineer, Yaeger didn't believe the "barrier" existed.[1]

You may be reading the above excerpt from *The Right Stuff* and wondering: what does breaking the sound barrier have to do with me? Actually, I would like to focus your attention on the man who did it: Chuck Yaeger.

The sound barrier was referred to as "a demon that lived in the air." Many men failed to conquer it and died trying. But Yaeger succeeded. One reason why, I think, is stated very simply in the second sentence:

"Not being an engineer, Yaeger didn't believe the 'barrier' existed."

We all have barriers to overcome. When I was in college, my barrier was getting a job and finding meaningful work. I was frustrated because I didn't think I could really accomplish anything while in school. I later realized that barrier to be, like many of those in our lives, non-existent in reality. *Barriers exist only within our own self-doubts and fears.*

This is one of the reasons why I wrote this book: to help you understand that many of the "barriers" or obstacles that you see standing between yourself and opportunity are often imagined.

Even better, the steps outlined in this book will help you discover the opportunities you can make for yourself. They can soften the transition and reduce your stress. They will put you in a better position to go out and earn a living, and to serve people in the capacity that you have been preparing for in school.

What Next? Here Are Some Steps You Can Take Today

1) If you don't keep a planner, get one. It doesn't have to be expensive, but it should feature a weekly calendar with sections for tracking names and contacts. It is also helpful to have a section where you can write down personal goals, and ideas you get which may be useful in future planning.

2) If you are not sure of what you want to do for a career, take a seminar or a short class in a subject or two which you find appealing.

3) Begin reading one book per month (after you have finished this one) that pertains, either directly or indirectly, to your professional goals.

4) If you are currently employed, look at your situation. Do you see an opportunity there that can increase your contribution? Identify one problem that exists and solve it. Be discreet as you go through this process. However, when you have accomplished it, be sure to let everyone know—without being obnoxious about it—who gets the credit.

3

The First Great Leap...
Volunteer!

"There is an element of risk, when we serve 'strangers.' Taking that step is one way communities are formed."

>   - Bobby Kapur
>   *Rice University*
>   *English/Pre-Medicine*

"Before you try to find a job, you must have an idea of what you do best," says Bobby Kapur. "It's always important to find out what your interests and strengths are. I believe that service can provide that opportunity."

Bobby worked with the Rice Student Volunteer Program (RSVP) during all four of his undergraduate years. He got involved with the OUTREACH program tutoring inner-city middle school students and, as an Eagle Scout with a local Boy Scout troop, he taught outdoor and leadership skills. Bobby served as RSVP Vice Chair and coordinated Outreach Day, a day of service involving 600 students and faculty with thirty different area service projects.

Furthermore, Bobby's leadership as a dormitory representative to the Health Education Office led him to help plan and promote educational programs on a broad range of health-related issues facing the

Rice community, and he helped coordinate Rice's Diversity Awareness Week with the Office of Multicultural Affairs.

A man of Asian-Indian descent, Bobby feels that communities cannot prosper without people serving one another. "Gandhi used an term, *Sarvodaya*, which expresses how we serve others throughout our lives. We start by serving ourselves, by providing basic needs. Then we serve our family and friends. Beyond that, there is an element of risk, when we serve 'strangers.' Taking that step is one way communities are formed."

Campus Outreach Opportunity League invited Bobby to join its board of directors as a result of his outstanding work with RSVP. After noting Bobby's exemplary service record, Rotary International awarded Bobby an Ambassadorial Scholarship and he served for one year as Ambassador of Goodwill to Australia.

Since his graduation from Rice, Bobby has continued his involvement in community service while studying at Baylor College of Medicine. During his first year of courses, Bobby volunteered in the pediatrics ward of Ben Taub County Hospital. He went on to become the Director of Community Service for the Baylor Student Association where he coordinates and encourages medical student involvement in community service initiatives.

"Many people fail to realize that when they give in their community, they get a whole lot in return," Bobby says. "Our society is such that we must be able to communicate and adapt to a wide variety of people, regardless of our profession. There are countless opportunities to serve even if just for a couple of hours a week, that will greatly broaden a student's horizons and capacity to work with and benefit others."

I mentioned earlier that as you prepare for a career, you are preparing to *serve others*. That's the basis for the *interdependence* of our global economy and world. It's inescapable. As you read this book, you are being served not only by myself, but the people who published it and those who sold it to you. Each time you turn on the lights, throw a frozen dinner into the microwave or go to sleep, you are being served by the time, talent and efforts of countless other people. If you plan on working in the non-profit sector, your entree into this area as a volunteer or intern may be very instrumental in gaining future work. If not, volunteering still offers many practical benefits.

Why Volunteer? *The World Needs You*

While your life is being improved and affected by others as you go about your day, you are most likely doing something to return the favor. Even as a student, your class attendance, participation and tuition fees go to the enrichment of other people's lives, like those of your instructors, the staff and other employees of your learning institution. In fact, the presence of a school or college does economic wonders for a community.

We cannot escape this concept of *interdependency*. We can receive a greater understanding of it, ourselves and our role in our community by *getting involved*.

Our World Needs People Who Care About Making It a Better Place

It is said that the best way to be successful is to "find a need and fill it." As you know, our society—*our world*—has many needs. Just turn on the news. You don't have to look very far to find needs in your community, or anywhere else.

Depressing? Well, despite ups and downs throughout our history, needs have always been here and will continue to be for some time.

Over the years, individuals have mobilized independently to cope with these ills and to make our lives better. The result is the wide range of non-profit organizations (also known as the *Third Sector*—the first and second being government and private business) we know today. Non-profits thrive and serve with the support of individuals, businesses and foundations who give their time and money. But even with the millions of people who volunteer at varied levels each year, there is still much need for your time, your talents and your services.

There are countless people right now who, if you gave them the chance, would eagerly tell you of the opportunities they have for your service—to tell you how much *they need you and your abilities.*

And here lies the opportunity of a lifetime: the chance to change many lives, *starting with your own.*

What Do You Get from Volunteering?

There are many benefits to be gained from volunteering, both for yourself and those you are serving. The benefits are both tangible and intangible—but most important is that they are *residual*. If you let them, they will continue to have a positive effect on you for the rest of your life.

1. *You serve others and yourself at the same time.*

When you give your time and talents—putting together the menu for a soup kitchen, doing publicity for a local advocacy group, watching children in a day care center or answering phones for the American Red Cross—you help yourself in many ways.

The first is by making your community a better place in which to live. Those served by your organization—whether they are elderly people who are shut in, men and women stricken with disease or children who have no place to call home—are the ones you benefit.

Take a visit to any service organization in your area, preferably one that has a highly visible impact. Count the volunteers. Ask yourself: *What would happen to my community if these people didn't take the time to care?*

What will happen to peoples' lives if **you** *don't?*

By taking action and getting involved, you not only improve the quality of life, you improve the economic interest people take in the area, thus beginning a cycle of stability and peace of mind for everyone. Furthermore, you can take pride in solutions you have developed and the good works you have done to help others.

2. *You build lasting relationships with other people.*

You have already heard a lot about the term **networking**. You have probably also asked yourself: *Just what is it?*

Networking—which we will discuss further in chapter 5—is much simpler than you may have read elsewhere. Excluding all "people strategies" and "how to work a room" tactics, at its heart, networking is simply the process of building relationships with other people.

Good News! Volunteering is one of the most effective ways to network! As a volunteer, you demonstrate your abilities, not only in your field, but as a communicator and a team player. Your commitment of time and energy to a good cause demonstrates a strong character ethic. *You have established your credibility amongst your colleagues and may have won some favors too.*

And instead of the usual hierarchy which you are likely to encounter in a business, at a volunteer organization, you often are perceived as an equal, regardless of your age or the level of your skills. Even more, you are openly appreciated for the time and effort you give, mainly because you could be doing something else—like sitting at home watching television.

Also consider this: people working together on a project or task in which they both believe is one of the strongest ways to build lasting relationships. When individuals whose lives are grounded in basic, timeless principles encounter another who appears to share those qualities, they tend to take a liking to them and feel a common bond or friendship.

As a result, it is also easier to stay in touch with those individuals, which is very important to building strong relationships, and thus, a strong network. By making an occasional phone call or clipping a noteworthy article out of a magazine and sending it to them, you foster a relationship that runs deeper than an occasional encounter at a superficial "social" gathering.

Later, we will examine the general political structure that many organizations tend to follow and how it can help you become connected in business, industry and government.

3. You enhance your expertise.

When I began as editor of the Columbus YWCA/IHN *Network News*, I had, despite my many years in marketing, communications and desktop publishing, very little experience in actual newsletter editing and production. The first couple of issues showed it! But the last few years as editor have vastly increased my editing capabilities and my software techniques. I have also enhanced my ability to communicate with others on what I need from them to complete the publication, which we now publish more frequently.

When you seek out volunteer opportunities you may, if you already have chosen your calling, be interested in work that helps to fulfill that calling. A journalism major might seek work involving public relations or communications for a homeless shelter. A student involved in education may be interested in working with children at a YMCA day-care center. An aspiring nurse may wish to get experience working with the sick through the Red Cross or with an AIDS advocacy group.

Just by starting out in the right direction you develop precision and skills that will be indispensable down the road.

4. *You develop skills that employers seek out universally, yet are not often found.*

In "What Small Firms Look for in New-Graduate Candidates," an article published in the *Journal of Career Planning and Employment*, the authors make some very clear distinctions as to what most employers examine:

•Skills, abilities and personal characteristics

•En .rgy, initiative, motivation and self-direction

•A team player with interpersonal and oral communication skills

Of less concern were items (a few to my surprise) traditionally found on resumes, such as leadership roles, creativity and written communication. *Of least importance were GPA and other academic credentials.*[1]

The great thing about volunteer work is that it can help you develop all of these attributes. Quite simply, volunteer work is the opportunity that you make of it.

Let's look at some of the top credentials that, according to these authors, employers look for. Remember: these are skills applicable to virtually *every* field of endeavor, so you can't look at any of them and say they don't apply to you.

Oral communication was one of the most sought-after skills. It is basically the ability to *carry out a conversation and convey yourself effectively, especially in some formal setting.* This is not a skill that comes easily to most, but with practice it can be developed.

What very common task often required of volunteers can help you develop this skill with fluent precision?

You know the answer: *telephone work*. Communicating with people over the phone is a great way to fine tune your ability to speak clearly and think on your toes.

Regarding *skills, abilities and personal characteristics*, we have already discussed how service work can help you develop specific skills of countless variety, be they technical or social. By building a track record and relationships within an organization that works for something you feel is important, you also reveal a piece of your *character*. This represents your values, your goals and how you align your life with basic fundamental principles. It lets others see you as a *person*, not just someone who wants a job.

This is important, because it lets others see you as a giver, as opposed to a "needy" job applicant.

Now let's examine *energy, initiative, motivation and self-direction*. One of the beauties of service work is the issue of choice. You choose the work that is important to you, and you take the initiative to make a difference. *To take such actions without the direction of someone else is an entrepreneurial trait that knocks the socks off employers.* They want a person who is a doer, and if that's you, then more power to you.

Nicholas Murray Butler said that people can be divided into three groups: "those who make things happen, those who watch things happen, and those who wonder what happened." This is your opportunity to define the group in which you belong.

While *leadership roles, creativity* and *written communication* were not ranked as high, they are still extremely important. If you demonstrate initiative and self-direction, you develop leadership qualities by default. Creativity is important when providing solutions to problems, and that is needed everywhere. This overlaps with the ability to write, and I will tell you that writing does not come easily, even to professionals. It is one of the most physically and mentally draining tasks one can do. It also takes years to really develop as a skill. You will read more about creativity later on.

5. You have greater choices and more flexibility.

We alluded to this point earlier. When you volunteer, you have the power to choose what work you wish to do and how much time to commit to it. Due to the wealth of opportunity for service work for college students, the competition for volunteers among non-profit organizations is strong. These organizations know that if they do not treat you right and give you the respect you deserve, then you can simply go serve somewhere else. And they don't want that.

As a result, non-profits are often very flexible about project and task assignments. They want you to contribute where you will get the most out of it and feel rewarded. This is also to their benefit, because then you are most likely to put forth your best efforts and add quality to your work.

6. You can try things you never have before.

Have you ever wondered how effective you might be at:

- Public speaking?
- Writing a brochure or an advertisement?
- Looking after a half-dozen toddlers for a morning?
- Listening to troubled, traumatized individuals?
- Cooking for large groups?
- Managing other individuals?
- Driving large vehicles?
- Teaching English or tutoring math?

The list could go on and on. **There is virtually no limit to the service opportunities and experience that volunteering can offer you!**

This is a chance to discover the gold mine within yourself, to really find out what you are capable of. Despite whatever weaknesses you may see in yourself, you most certainly are qualified to perform some tasks and the opportunity is there.

In Columbus, Ohio, we have a local organization known as FIRST-LINK. It serves as a "clearing house" for those who wish to volunteer. You call their office, give them your name and address, interests and the time levels you are able and willing to commit.

The people at FIRSTLINK enter your answers into a computer database. Then, over the telephone and often in a matter of minutes, they give you a list of all the service opportunities that match your interests. They will also provide a complete list of names and phone numbers.

When I first contacted FIRSTLINK, I was looking for opportunities in marketing communications such as in public relations or in advertising. **Within a week, I received a set of printouts that spelled out over forty organizations and contacts who needed my help, and were willing to train!**

The point is, if you have an interest, you really have nothing to lose by giving it a try. In many organizations, free volunteer training sessions exist to teach new skills that you can apply to your service, and later on, to your career.

7. *You will improve your self-esteem and be appreciated.*

Employees often become disillusioned with their work when they do not think they are appreciated. Their employers don't make them feel as though they are needed. Sure, most companies brag that their employees are "their greatest resource," but that attitude usually doesn't get past the lip service.

What it comes down to is what we talked about in the first chapter: people are sometimes treated as a commodity. They are an asset to be bought when needed and to be let go when not. I'm not asserting the morality of such an attitude, but it is the reality of business today and tomorrow as well.

Most people's work has some bearing on the lives of others. How apparent that is to the employee varies greatly. But service work can offer a variety of opportunities for you to see the difference you make in people's lives.

In the Frank Capra movie, *It's a Wonderful Life*, Jimmy Stewart's character George Bailey, in a moment during an intense personal struggle, wishes he had never lived. He states in anguish that the world would be a whole lot better had he never been born.

Clarence, his guardian angel, gives him that opportunity: to see a world in which he had never lived. The result is a dark picture, where

people he had known and loved led entirely different and less meaningful lives.

At the risk of being overly sentimental, the message of this
movie is very clear: in the most subtle way, you have the potential to
greatly improve your own life and the lives of others. As a result you
will, as George Bailey found out at the end of the film, be paid back in
multitudes.

**By seeing the difference you make for other people, by hear-
ing how much you are appreciated, your self-esteem will thrive.**
Your self-esteem is very important. It affects your relationships, and
your relationships have a great bearing on your success in life, in both
your work and your family.

8. *You may take on greater challenges than you will in an entry-level job.*

Often, fewer people assume more responsibility in smaller, non-
profit organizations. When groups are tight on resources, they are
eager to give a qualified person willing to take on a compelling project or responsibility a chance.

A few years ago, I met with some people who were serving in a
local chapter of UNICEF, the well-known, *worldwide* relief organization focused on the needs of children. This local chapter was a small
group with many responsibilities, primarily raising money through
fund-raising events, school projects involving local children, and running a card and stationary store. This was almost entirely accomplished through the help of volunteers.

When I met them, they were eager to have someone volunteer
to serve as a public relations chair. This was because, despite their
many successful efforts in fund-raising, they still did not have the "public" presence they deemed necessary to advance the cause of helping
impoverished children around the globe.

In our conversations, I asked if they would be open to having a
college student come in and help the group with publicity. Their
response was positive—they would be delighted to work with a young
person who was willing to make a commitment to help them achieve
their goal.

What an opportunity! This was a small chapter of a huge organization, with plenty of support and name recognition. And it offered a lot more responsibilities and challenges than what you would typically find in an entry-level job!

9. Service can help you choose your vocation.

If you are like most students, you may have already changed your major course of study at least once. I studied graphic and advertising design for two-and-a-half years before I decided to pursue a degree in journalism. For me, that involved switching schools. Let's hope that if you change, it's not such a hassle. But don't avoid the change if it is. It's important that your lifelong career be one that challenges and suits you.

If you do have second thoughts about what you want to do, remember that it's normal. Experts are now saying that most adults will change *their careers* up to seven times over their lifetime! So don't worry. Change is natural.

As I mentioned earlier, service work can help you try new things. In the same manner, it can help you reaffirm or reconsider a decision regarding your vocation. It may not give you the opportunity to actually work that job you are hoping to get, but it may allow you to gain insight on how you might handle that type of occupation.

For instance, Connie, a long-time friend of my sister originally enrolled in college as a nursing student. She rationalized that since she was always the one who cared for other people, then nursing would be a good occupation for her.

While in school Connie started volunteering at a local hospital, working alongside many of the nurses whom she hoped to join professionally in a couple of years. In doing so, she made some very startling discoveries about herself. It turned out Connie couldn't stand the sight of blood, nor was she able to cope very well with people who were experiencing intense physical pain.

That's kind of significant if you plan to be a nurse, isn't it? Connie thought so. Her service gave her the opportunity to see her own limitations. And she felt fortunate to have discovered these limitations early on.

The important thing to remember is that even if you may not be able to perform the exact functions you would in a professional position, service work can still allow you to decide whether or not a particular vocation is right for you. There are countless ways to serve. Find something that best suits what you think you might want to do for a living and give it a try.

Also realize that it is as equally important to understand your own weaknesses, as it is to know your strengths and true ambitions.

10. You can learn by seeing things from others' perspectives.

A few years ago, whenever things were not going the way I wanted, I would begin to feel sorry for myself. Then I would tell myself, "No matter how bad things get for me, there is always someone else who's got it worse."

This may not always be comforting, but it is true.

Depending upon your areas of service, you may encounter people whose immense problems make yours seem insignificant. I know that I did. When I was unemployed for a few months, I often felt sorry for myself, thinking that my problems were about as bad as they could get. But my experience volunteering through my church to help homeless families allowed me to meet and work with people who had it far worse than I ever did. These were *families* who had no homes. These people had so much less than I had. They came in from the streets carrying everything they owned in a few bags.

Many of you reading this book may now or will in the future experience hardships of some kind, be they personal problems with relationships, employment or finances. Some of you might grapple with substance abuse, or mental or physical ailments. **You should also know, intellectually at least, that no matter how hard your problems, you are not alone.** I am not a trained counselor or therapist, but I do know from experience that serving others, some of whom may have similar problems to the ones you might be struggling with—and in many cases far worse—may be some of the best therapy you can prescribe for yourself. You may even come across a person who can help you.

Overcoming personal adversity is something we all must face at one time or another to varying degrees. I believe that by working with others who might be less fortunate, you can learn to put your own problems in perspective and not let them prevent you from taking action to help others and yourself.

Volunteering will help you improve your attitude and overall emotional well-being. You will come to appreciate what you have, as well as what you can offer. You will become a better person, with a stronger idea of what you want out of your life.

This idea was best described by the late Dr. Norman Vincent Peale.[2] As he observed in his book, *The Power of the Plus Factor*, by taking the time to care for other people, you will, in his words, "discover the key that unlocks the door to real happiness."

As you will recall from Bobby Kapur's story at the start of the chapter, Bobby received several of the benefits I have listed. By volunteering his time and reaching out to his community, he met many people and improved his skills in communicating and in being more adaptable. He developed a sense of pride in his work and in his ability to help others. Even better, when other groups like Rotary International and Campus Outreach Opportunity League recognized Bobby's achievements, they opened up new doors for Bobby by giving him a goodwill ambassadorship and a seat on a board of directors.

Bobby's initial venture into serving his community led him to greater challenges and opportunities than he ever expected. If this can happen for Bobby, then it can happen for you, too. Just don't wait!

What Next? Some Steps You Can Take *Today*

1) Visit a local non-profit organization, such as a Red Cross or YMCA (see Appendix I). Talk to some of the volunteers about their choices of service and the relationships which developed. Let them tell you their stories.

2) Contact a local volunteer clearinghouse and find out what kind of opportunities may exist. You will be amazed at how many there are. A great number offer professional-level experience!

3) As you follow the guidelines in this book, you will meet many influential people. Ask them about their community service experiences and what role they have played in their personal and professional development.

4) What is the one professional skill—such as public speaking, planning projects or computer knowledge—which you believe would have the most impact on your career? Seek out a specific volunteer or internship opportunity which would allow you to develop, exercise and improve that skill.

4

Where to Find
Service Opportunities

*"The city was my backyard, and that was where I saw the opportunity
to serve."*

- Jennifer Appleton
University of Southern California
Health and Human Services

The University of Southern California is located in an inner-city
area of Los Angeles. Many people view this as negative and detrimen-
tal to USC's image. Jennifer Appleton, however, thought the urban
location was the most important aspect of her experience as an undergraduate.

During her time at the university, Jennifer found many volunteer
opportunities in the inner-city. She taught art to local, developmen-
tally-disabled teenagers, served as a teacher's aide at 32nd Street
Elementary School and organized events on campus for pre-school
children from the city.

In addition, Jennifer helped found, staff and develop the new USC
Student Volunteer Center, spoke at conferences for Youth Service

America, the Points of Light Foundation, Campus Outreach Opportunity League, and Learning Through Service and helped in developing the AmeriCorps program.

A strong advocate of service in education, Jennifer feels that the students benefit in many ways. "Service is not about adding a line to a resume," she says. "It's not like just putting in your time somewhere and taking credit for it. How does someone get to *know you* from that? Through service, we do something we cannot do in mere words. We communicate to other people *who we are* and what an experience means to us."

"Early in school, don't concern yourself too much with what career you want to go into. Begin discovering your own skills and talents, what you are good at. That could be art, business, communicating with others or working with children—anything. Where can those skills be used so you can fine tune them and help others at the same time? This will help you discover who you are and how you can contribute to a better world."

Upon graduation, Jennifer's record of service enabled her to get her first job at the Constitutional Rights Foundation, a Los Angeles-based non-profit organization which assists middle and high school students in identifying the roots of community problems, such as unemployment, gangs and broken families. Some of the programs to solve these problems include inter-generational and peer tutoring, police ride-along programs and public park and neighborhood refurbishment. "As a result of this work, I can tell you story after story of kids whose lives were changed after taking charge of and changing their own neighborhood."

This work led to her job as a policy analyst in the U.S. Department of Health and Human Services, where she combined her educational background and community service experience to pursue her goal of making a difference in the lives of those in need.

Her advice to college students: "The city was my backyard, and that was where I saw my opportunity to serve. Participating in the community surrounding USC provided me with my most meaningful experiences in college. My service-related experiences at USC inspired me to pursue a career in which I could continue to positively impact urban communities, as well as inspire others to be involved in this pursuit."

Where to Start

Jennifer knew she wanted to help her community, and she found one which definitely needed her help. If you're interested in volunteering, but unlike Jennifer, are not sure where to find the people who need your services, allow me to offer some suggestions.

Volunteer Clearinghouses

Before I discuss the different kinds of organizations that exist and the types of services you can perform, let's revisit the heart of the issue.

Remember, you are searching for needs. You may have an idea of the kinds of services and talents you can offer, or you may be pretty open to learning new skills.

This is why blanket volunteer clearinghouses can be a great start. Remember how I got more than forty opportunities sent to me for public relations work when I filled out an interest form for FIRST**LINK**?

Volunteer clearinghouses serve their area's non-profit organizations by matching talented people with others who can use their services. They may send you a comprehensive interest form, in which you list (often from a selection provided) your interests and talents. They then plug that data into a computer, which matches it up to local organizational needs.

I have listed some of the names, phone numbers and addresses for several clearinghouses in appendix I. Remember to check for more in your local yellow pages.

Non-profit Organizations: Six Categories

For our purposes, I have divided non-profit organizations into six major categories. By doing this, we can home in on what interests you, as well as where you can serve these interests. The categories are:

1) Social/Community Service
2) Cultural/Arts
3) Educational

4) Political and Advocacy

5) Business, Trade, and Professional

6) Religious

Some organizations may have overlapping programs and services. For instance, a social service agency, such as an AIDS support
group, may have advocacy programs hoping to influence legislation or
its constituents. Likewise, business organizations may have similar
projects and many political groups have this as their sole agenda. One
thing they all have in common: they need you.

Social/Community Service Organizations

Often, this is what people tend to think of most when they hear
the term "non-profit." This group consists of individual homeless
shelters, food banks, volunteer centers, non-government child-welfare
agencies, as well as multinational organizations such as the Red Cross,
the Salvation Army (although the Salvation Army is actually a church
organization—again there is the overlap) and the YMCA.

We may include hospitals in this group as well. While there are
some hospitals in this country that operate for a profit, most are non-
profit. They, too, are involved in many forms of community service
beyond direct health care, and a significant number have religious affil-
iation. Hospitals also have a great need for volunteers.

These organizations were often developed in response to a crisis
or to problems of some kind, and are dedicated to the eventual elimi-
nation of those problems.

A more comprehensive list of some organizations which operate
nationally, and may have a chapter in your neighborhood, is found in
appendix I.

Cultural/Arts Organizations

Does your town have a symphony orchestra? An art museum? A
community theater? Do you have a cultural arts center near the college where people can take art classes, such as ceramics and painting,
in the evenings? How about your public library?

If your college town has any of these, then chances are they operate as non-profit organizations. Nearly all do. Most utilize volunteers for developing new programs, teaching classes and fund raising.

The work available to volunteers can vary greatly. You may be able to help in administrative tasks, working with a particular department, planning events or just helping with custodial or maintenance duties. Theaters often use volunteers for ushering and ticketing. Public broadcasting stations nearly always have volunteers answering their phones during fund drives. Libraries often need support in community outreach programs.

Educational Organizations

Schools, colleges and universities are mostly non-profit organizations, many of which are private, with little or no government funding. What kind of volunteer support a school or college may seek depends highly on that institution.

Many schools offer programs and activities that go beyond their standard curricula. These may include tutoring, after-school latchkey programs (often sponsored by a YMCA or other local organization), clubs and sporting events.

Of course, most school administrators and teachers will acknowledge that they can always use help on the playgrounds, in the classrooms and in their libraries.

There is a growing trend of increased cooperation between business and education today, where individuals occasionally come out of their daily workplace to take part in vocational guidance or other forms of enrichment programs for students. This includes professionals talking with students about their jobs. It can also mean assisting a teacher in class instruction regarding a particular topic, such as finance, computers, or applied sciences.

If you currently attend college, then you have no doubt been exposed to many on- and off-campus programs, groups and activities. Some may be directly sponsored by your college, and others may not. While much of their volunteer help may come from alumni, and other departments may use graduate or scholarship students, you may have some specific skills that are useful in tutoring or supporting a campus project. The opportunities may be right under your nose.

Political and Advocacy Organizations

When we talk of political organizations, we are not just referring to the Republican or Democratic parties. There are other organizations which build awareness and work on political advocacy for human rights, the environment and other issues that impact our lives. Many run ongoing campaigns and are in constant search of speakers, letter writers and people who can answer questions over the phone.

Here they seek people who truly believe in their message, who feel *passionately* about it. Often, that requirement outweighs any other personal qualifications. If you are truly passionate about a specific agenda, goal or ideal, and can communicate that passion, then you can be useful to that organization. It can be a great opportunity to further something you believe in, and, at the same time, build solid communication skills which will be helpful to you in your future career.

Political or electoral campaigns would also be found under this category. Many people use these campaigns to help them slip into jobs in areas they feel strongly committed to. On a national level, National Public Radio reported that, shortly after Bill Clinton's election to the presidency, he received a ton of resumes from people who worked on getting him elected. They were now seeking positions in his administration.

This also happens at the local level, and often people will back a candidate as much (or more) for the job opportunity it may offer as for their belief in the candidate's values and agenda.

Although this strategy can be a beneficial one, it has two drawbacks. First, you could put your blood, sweat and tears into a campaign, only to have your candidate lose. Second, you often have a job only as long as your candidate does.

Regardless of how your candidate performs, by participating, you still will have built needed skills and developed some solid relationships. And if you believe that your agenda and candidate is of true benefit to society, then you did your best to make a difference in your community, and it was worth-while to seize the opportunity.

Business/Trade/Professional Organizations

Do you have your sights set on a particular occupation or industry? Wouldn't it be great to have an opportunity to work for and become well acquainted with the people who work in these fields?

There are thousands of organizations, most of which are non-profit and primarily volunteer-driven, that cater to people who have particular interests or occupations, or want to work within a certain industry. *Each of these organizations is a fantastic resource to gain knowledge and experience and to start building relationships with other committed people who may help you.*

Pay a visit to your local library and take a look at the *Encyclopedia of Associations*. This is a huge volume that covers a good percentage of organizations across the country that cater to different career fields. The *Encyclopedia* also publishes supplementary volumes that contain state, regional and local organizations with which you may wish to begin.

As large as it is and comprehensive as it attempts to be, this book may not list all of the associations which actually exist in your area. Many libraries collect this information on their own and may have a more complete listing. Ask your librarian if there is anything available.

Volunteer and internship opportunities, like anything else, can vary widely. In many organizations there may be a paid executive director and no one else, which means that a single person juggles a lot of responsibilities and thus might rely on volunteer assistance. The type of work may not be glamorous, involving, in many cases, answering phones and stuffing envelopes. If you demonstrate other abilities and ways to be valuable, sooner or later that important need will arise and you will be the one within the director's arm's length to fill it.

Serving this way gives you the opportunity to gain real knowledge about a field you may be considering and to connect with others. The board members, as with other non-profits, are often made up of highly experienced professionals. Often they are well-connected and are serving on the board as volunteers. Either way, by volunteering, you are working for them and thus building a great foundation for future relationships and perhaps employment, as well as future opportunities to serve.

If you are considering a professional organization which pertains to your field, consider volunteering for one of that organization's volunteer leaders. Presidents, treasurers and secretaries often have rotating terms and are often volunteer positions. A busy professional who is serving in this capacity may welcome the help of a student in planning events and organizing speakers, and just making phone calls to association members is a good way to meet people.

If you think this may be a route to take, make your pilgrimage to the library and look at the directories available. Make a list of those worth considering and follow up, inquiring about their need for volunteer help. This type of volunteer work could lead to many great opportunities.

Religious Organizations

Religious organizations not only consist of churches, synagogues and mosques, but the regional groups that they belong to, such as a diocese or regional conference. For our purpose, we will focus mainly on the individual religious organization and how it uses volunteers.

Did you know that more than 70 percent of all philanthropic giving in the United States today is to religious institutions?

If you currently attend a church or synagogue regularly, you may not be aware of the volunteer opportunities that may exist. Many churches, for example, are involved in much more than having their members congregate for weekly services. Often, churches and synagogues successfully position themselves as community centers, opening their doors to other worthy groups in the area. Most religious organizations are active in various forms of outreach, meaning that they lend their financial and human support to directly serve the community. One example is the many churches that operate food banks by collecting and storing donated canned and dry goods and distributing them to those who need them.

There are many other ways religious organizations are involved in outreach. Some will offer evening classes on a wide variety of topics, such as personal finance, parenting and personal communication, in addition to those related to faith. Others offer counseling and have programs in which their members regularly volunteer and support existing community outreach programs.

If you have a religious faith of some kind, and perhaps belong to a church or synagogue, but have not really explored the ways in which you can become more involved now that you are a college student, then it is really something you may want to consider. Most religious organizations operate on the 80/20 rule. That is, 80 percent of the financial and human support comes from 20 percent of its members. When you look at this ratio, you can see how much talent and human resource is virtually untapped.

If you don't have a particular religious faith, you should not let that hinder you if you feel compelled to support a religious-sponsored program or activity. Official membership is rarely a concern, and most of these groups welcome visitors of all backgrounds and beliefs.

The opportunities available for service in these organizations can involve virtually all aspects of administration, such as committee work, finance, fundraising and communications. Whatever an individual church or other institution is involved in, there is bound to be opportunity for you to serve.

Should You Volunteer?

I hope that after reading the previous chapter and this one, your answer to this is a resounding "Yes!" But it is a question you will have to answer for yourself. There are some points which you must still keep in mind before making this decision.

What Do You Really Care About?

Don't feel obligated to jump right into the first opportunity that comes along, unless you really feel strongly about it in your heart. These are decisions that are more often based upon emotion than logic, and justly so.

The best way to avoid a situation of bad commitment is to ask yourself a simple question: *What do I care about?*

As we discussed earlier, we live in a world with a lot of problems and needs. There are thousands of non-profit organizations in this country. Most were started by an individual or group of individuals who felt emotionally drawn to meeting a particular need.

In many cases, the founders took notice of a particular problem and became angry. They used their anger to do something constructive.

For me, homelessness, especially that of children, is a big issue. When I became a parent, I realized that all children are no different from my own, and all deserve nurturing. That's one thing I really care about.

In asking yourself to consider what you really care about, you have to start somewhere. Your passion may not be homelessness. It may be the environment, racism, illiteracy, an incurable disease or saving abandoned and abused animals. Maybe you have a passion for improving our government and the political system or a desire to become a living example of your faith.

Don't be surprised if your concern is tied to something that has affected your life somehow. It may have touched you or someone you know directly. Many people who have gotten angry about a problem in our society have done so as a result of being affected personally.

The reason why you MUST feel emotionally drawn to an issue is so you will have the inspiration and the heart to serve your very best. You will give and receive to your fullest potential. A half-hearted commitment, or an agreement to do something merely because you were asked to, may not best serve the organization's or your own needs. In fact, it can do more harm than good.

So when you come across an organization or group of people you may wish to serve and connect with, take your time and don't rush it. Introduce yourself and let them know you are interested in volunteering. Find out what their needs are and what goals they work to accomplish. Become acquainted with those people you will be working with. Do you like them? Do you feel a certain fellowship with them?

These are important questions to answer, because you are making a commitment, and you are doing it of your own free will. You should really like those you are working with. When you start a full-time job, you will be forced to work with many people you may not like or at least don't get along with. Don't let that dilemma carry over into your volunteer service. That will take the fun out if it. Think about who you are really serving and be sure you want to help this group of people.

Benefit Others–Benefit Yourself

As the saying goes, the hungry man who foolishly plants a packet of seeds expecting to eat dinner that evening is destined to remain hungry. Just remember that if you go into a volunteer relationship expecting it to lead directly to a job, you will most likely be disappointed. There is no direct, sure-fire path to a job. However, most jobs, as you should know by now, are gained through personal relationships. And those relationships take time to nurture. By volunteering with others and accomplishing tasks which you care about, your good character will inevitably help you to attract and develop friendships which will stand the test of time.

Be Careful Not to Overcommit

Chances are, especially if you are new, that whatever commitment you make will require more time than you anticipate. So when starting out, be conservative. The last thing you want to do is commit so much time to a task that you cannot get it done, or finish the task only at the expense of your studies. Also, if you don't come through on your responsibilities, this hurts both you and those you are serving.

Set a Tangible Goal for the Organization and Yourself

When we volunteer, we do so to make a difference, preferably one that we can see and benefit from. It's important to set specific goals which serve specific needs. If you are volunteering and don't feel any real contribution, search for the needs. Look for an opportunity to solve a problem, start a program and increase the group's level of service.

After all, you don't want a resume of past jobs. You want a resume of past *accomplishments*.

Evaluate what the specific needs of the organization are, along with their objectives or mission. This is important. How are they fulfilling that mission? In what ways can you improve that service? Do they have a dire need of some kind that is not being filled? Most non-profit organizations do. Go in and ask them, "What can I do?" or "How can I help?" They will most likely say, "Pull up a chair," and immediately begin to tell you just how much you are needed.

If the organizational structure of the group permits it, evaluate the organization's and corresponding community's needs against your capabilities and resources. Working with them, realistically decide upon and verbally commit to filling a specific necessity of the organization and, subsequently, the people it serves. If you think it is appropriate and necessary, write out a plan for doing so, including your specific role and everyone else's, that spells out the goal and the course to get there. **Make this suggestion: "I see that you have this problem, and here is what I think I can do to help you solve it."**

I'm not saying that you should burst through the doors of a service organization and tell them that you are taking charge, or even automatically assume a position of leadership. When initiating what you hope becomes a long and fulfilling relationship, that is the last thing you want to do. Accept that, at first, your role or visibility may be small, but you will still be serving a vital purpose. Keep your long-term goal in mind and look for opportunities to fulfill it within the organization.

Remember Murphy's Law

Now suppose your plans, for whatever reason, do not seem to be working out as you had expected? If your efforts are consistent and sincere, don't worry about being branded a failure. Rarely does anything in life pan out just the way we hope. Make changes to your plan as you progress and always communicate with those with whom you are working. Most organizational leaders feel that a step in the right direction is far better than no step at all. Even if you do not produce the results you wish in the time you had hoped, you have still brought a vision for the future one step closer to becoming reality.

Never Quit

Once you have found your niche in the service arena and have begun building those relationships, don't let it go. You will eventually find a job or start a business that takes more of your time. You will have to balance it even more if you have a family. But stay involved and stay connected. You may have to cut back your time commitment, and that's okay. Chances are if you create a role for yourself that is meaningful, fulfilling, and beneficial to others, it will continue to be rewarding personally and helpful to your work as well. If a volunteer position starts to feel like a job, then you may wish to reconsider other ways you can serve.

What Next? Here Are Some Steps You Can Take *Today*

1) Contemplate the types of groups and organizations that need you. Use the list in appendix I in the back of this book. Look through your yellow pages, at the brochures of your church or synagogue and within your community. The opportunities are everywhere.

2) Clearly examine yourself and your values. Honestly ask yourself, "Why do I wish to volunteer?", "What do I truly care about?", "In what specific ways can I help people?" and "How much time can I afford to give?"

3) Visit non-profit organizations in your area. If you can, "interview" them. Make a list of what their *specific* needs are. If you examine the "needs," you may find your choices a bit easier. What needs exist which you are most capable of filling?

4) Once you find a good position within an organization, keep your word and view a volunteer responsibility with equal weight as you should that of job. This is something not to be

overstressed. Here is a tip Stephen Covey offers that will help you maintain this, as well as your relationships with others as you volunteer: *make promises sparingly.* When you make a promise be 100 percent sure you can keep it. This way, your word is solid and your integrity with others is more secure.

5) When you make the choice in favor of performing a volunteer service, remember that there are very few risks involved. If you feel that a certain service opportunity isn't turning out the way you expect, then move on to something else. Two things to remember if you do this: if you quit, do so in a manner that shows respect for the concerns of the organization. Don't just suddenly walk out on them. The other factor to remember is your own expectations. Why specifically did you not feel satisfied with this opportunity? Were your expectations too high? Should you be looking at a whole different field of service?

The Two Faces
of Networking

*"I remember a woman who came to me through a contact. She wanted to get together and have lunch...But it was so glaringly apparent at the time that my only value to her was **what I could do for her.**"*
- Adam Behrman
University of Virginia
Political and Social Thought

How does one build relationships which go deeper than mere acquaintanceships? As an undergraduate, Adam Behrman volunteered all four years at Madison House, UVA's student service organization which annually coordinates over 3,000 students in weekly service. In this role, Adam got to know people—*and became known to them*—throughout different parts of the community.

To Adam, service was not just a means to meet people, but also a way to find his calling in life. Adam served as a role model and friend to an at-risk youth through the Big Sibling program. When matched with a boy named Turung, Adam met with the boy's family. "I was moved when Turung's little sister came up to me and asked me if I was her big brother too," Adam recalls. "It was then, and over the two years that followed, that I realized the overwhelming need for volunteers."

From that point, Adam became the first training director for the Big Sibling program. He also established and led retreats for all Madison House student leaders, focusing on individual growth, leadership and community development.

Upon his graduation in 1985, Adam went on to obtain a graduate degree in Counseling Psychology. He currently has a private practice in Berkeley, California. In addition, Adam founded "Discovery," a men's weekend retreat that was incorporated into a non-profit organization. He also leads retreats and training workshops across the United States and abroad, focusing on the needs of individuals and organizations and how they relate to one another.

Regarding networking, Adam offers this advice: "How you relate to others when you meet them can make a big difference in building relationships. Networking is a big part of what I do, because it's how I get most of my clients."

"One of the big problems I have seen in networking is that often there is a tendency to view people not as *people*, but as resources to be used," Adam adds. "I remember distinctly a woman who came to me through a contact. She wanted to get together and have lunch and pick my brain. But it was so glaringly apparent at the time that my only value to her was *what I could do for her*. That was a turn-off for me. The way in which we relate to others in these meetings is so very important. You don't want people to think that you are merely using them. You are initiating a relationship."

Part of Adam's success today, both in his private practice and in the creation of "Discovery," is due to his ability to network. Networking, when done correctly, can be a valuable way to promote yourself, as well as your career. But before you try this on your own, you must understand what networking is really all about.

Understanding the Difference Between
Building Contacts and Building Relationships

Networking has many definitions. The concept starts with simply meeting people and jotting down the names of everyone you know. You could call that your network. However, the next step is to ask yourself, does your list mean anything to you? How well do you know these people? Are any of them in a position to help you?

More importantly, are YOU in the position to help THEM? Ask yourself these questions:

1) How did we meet?

2) When was I last in touch with them?

3) Is there any basis for an on-going relationship?

So much that has been written about networking deals with *making contacts*. This is, in essence, collecting names. Business organizations and chambers of commerce hold social gatherings for this very purpose, so that business people can gather, talk and socialize, and pass out business cards. These events can be useful, and many productive relationships begin this way. However, there is also a certain superficiality behind some of them, much as there is found in the pickup bars or singles scenes which may exist on a college campus.

When two people connect, each might be wondering what the other can do for him or her. They chit-chat about business and trade cards. But unless there is some real rapport, they move on to the next target.

Much of what has been written in other books regarding networking deals with this: building contacts. The aim is to collect other people's names and get your name out.

This objective is important, but is too often overstressed and overrated, because the techniques and steps required to achieve this are easy to explain and simple to follow. Many books and articles vary somewhat in how they recommend going about it, but the bottom line is the same. The goal is to become acquainted and share information with as many people as possible.

Yet there is more to real networking than collecting names or finding ways to keep in touch with people. As a matter of fact, I favor a different expression altogether over the term networking, and I think it will benefit you if you think of it this way, as well. I call it, quite simply, *building relationships*.

It takes more than just passing out business cards to build relationships. It requires more than an occasional phone call, a holiday greeting card or remembering the names of another person's family members whom you've never met. Building relationships is a long-term goal, whereas building contacts is often regarded as, although mistakenly, a short-term goal.

Obviously, building relationships takes more time, and it requires more work. You cannot possibly build as many deep, lasting relationships in your about-to-be-if-not-already-busy life as you may be able to cram names into your phone book or palm pilot.

However, one good friend is often worth more than dozens of names of people whom you barely know and with whom you have little in common.

In essence, we are speaking of **quality over quantity**. It is an old theme, to be sure. However, in my own research I have not found it applied very often to the topic of networking.

Building Contacts or Relationships...
What Should You Do?

Does this mean that contacts are completely unhelpful? No. If you have ever stopped and asked a stranger for directions, then you know that even a casual acquaintance can point be helpful. As we will see from the next section about informational interviews, contacts can sometimes be great sources of information for you in your job hunt.

Just keep in mind that as you make these contacts, this is only the first step. The next is to turn these acquaintances into friends; to turn these connections into relationships.

So you must work on building both contacts and relationships. But before we talk more about developing relationships, let me share with you my adventures of making contacts, the most visible and elemental part of networking.

Building Contacts: The Author's Version

I said that everyone has their own version of what it takes to build contacts. For example, in his book *Sharkproof*, author Harvey Mackay says that to build contacts, you start with who you know. If you belong to a club or fraternity, every member, nationwide, is a contact worth calling. He says that you should collect five contacts a day.[1]

Well, that's possible, but it's tough. When you are a student with school and study responsibilities, and are about to call on a complete stranger—who is probably busy—and ask them for their time, you had better have a strong means of linking yourself to them.

One is that you might belong to a common professional organization. But your involvement in that organization may be much stronger than theirs. You volunteer, you go to the meetings, you even help plan them.

But other members may not be as involved, or they might not share in your enthusiasm for the organization. They may only belong because their employer requires it. You just don't know. So don't be surprised if you call upon a fellow member and their response is, "Yeah, we are both members. So what?"

Usually, though, the strongest connection is another human being.

One of the most common processes used in networking is what we call the *informational interview*. It is a simple meeting between two or more individuals to share information, insights, opinions, advice and *names*.

Before I became employed, I went on informational interviews far more often than job interviews.

They usually began with a phone call.

The First Phone Call

I sat down at my phone, pulled out the contact's number and stared at it. Taking up my script, I made sure that it was in front of me when I reached this person on the phone. Unsteadily, my fingers dialed the number.

The phone rang a few times. Then the receptionist answered. I immediately asked for Mr. Owens. Within thirty seconds, a voice came on:

"Tom Owens."

"Mr. Owens," I responded with a silent, yet hard swallow. "Thank you for taking my call. My name is Keith Luscher, and Rebecca Williams at Chase National Bank suggested I get in touch with you. Do you have just a few minutes?"

There was a moment of silence over the phone. Did he recognize my identified source for his name? Perhaps I was catching him at a bad moment or...

"I suppose," he responded. "What can I do for you?"

"Well," I said, looking to my cheat sheet, "I am a student pursuing a career in business communications and have been actively connecting with other individuals in the business community to share ideas and..."

I heard Mr. Owens give a slow sigh to himself as I continued with my pitch.

"...and while Ms. Williams said that your company may not be hiring, she did point out that you may be someone to speak with for information on the industry, and perhaps some solid advice in obtaining an internship, and eventually finding permanent work."

"Well," he responded, "she is right. We don't have any positions open right now. What did you say you do?"

"I am majoring in public relations. However, most of my experience so far has been in marketing communications and publishing," I said.

I could almost hear Mr. Owens' thoughts in that long moment of silence. I don't have time for this nonsense, he thought. I have too much to do as it is. Why did what's-her-name give this bozo my name and number in the first place?

"I'll tell you what," Mr. Owens said. "Send me your resume, and I'll look it over. If I hear of anything, I'll let you know."

Despite my disappointment, I tried to sound thankful for his time. "Thank you," I replied with gratitude. "I'll be happy to do that. I appreciate you taking my call, and I will get some information out to you in today's mail."

"Yeah, fine. Goodbye."

He hung up without waiting for my response.

If you find yourself engaged in informational interviewing, you will no doubt have negative phone conversations like this one. They can mean a couple of things about the person you are calling, including:

1) It has been a long time since this person was in a situation of having to look for work or make contacts and they react to those who make them negatively.

2) He or she is basically a considerate person and you are catching them on a bad day or at an inconvenient time.

This is a brief illustration of how badly some of my calls went. You can now listen in on how another one went:

With script in hand, I heard the phone ringing. The receptionist answered, and I asked to speak with Ms. Sharon Brown. She wasn't in, so I left a message with my name and number, and I pointed out to the receptionist that Rebecca Williams gave me Ms. Brown's name. I specifically asked that piece of information to be included in the message.

A few hours later, the phone rang. I answered it.

"Hello, may I speak with Keith Luscher?"

"Speaking."

"Hello, Keith. This is Sharon Brown returning your call," the voice said so politely.

I energized myself and my voice, trying to convey anticipation and enthusiasm. "Yes! Hello! Thank you so much for returning my call."

"No problem," she responded. "What can I do for you?"

"Well," I answered, "I really don't want to take too much of your time. I was just speaking with Rebecca Williams over at Chase the other day, and she suggested that I give you a call. I am a student pursuing a career in business and marketing communications. I have been touching base with different people in the business community, seeking opportunities for a position or an internship. Ms. Williams suggested that you would be an excellent person with whom to share ideas and perhaps to give some advice as well."

"Oh, okay, I would be happy to," she answered. "Would you like to meet sometime next week?"

"That would be great. What time is most convenient?"

"How's Wednesday at 10:00 a.m.?"

"At your office?"

"That will be fine. Why don't you bring a copy of your resume and some samples of your work?"

"I'll be there. Thanks again for returning my call," I concluded.
"See you then," she responded.

These are two opposite examples of responses. Indeed, there were many nuances. Some conversations went just as these two examples had. A few went on a bit longer with more conversation. But I did find that there was a great variance in how receptive people were to my call, which in turn depended upon a few other key factors, not all within my control.

Sometimes it was just simple timing. I often found that the best time to call an individual was just after five o'clock. That's usually when the gatekeepers have left the office but most of the decision-makers are still around, and the atmosphere is more relaxed.

However, no matter what time you call someone, especially when you know them and are hoping to connect, there is the chance that you will get them at a bad moment. You must try to remain sensitive to that. When you first get the person on the line, ask if there would be a more convenient time to contact them. As I said earlier, if you get someone who is not eager to speak with you, it may simply be due to more pressing demands of the moment. *Don't ever assume that once a person answers their phone they have time to talk.*

One other factor is that many people, believe it or not, *do not understand the concept of networking.* Even if, as a student, you just want to meet people and are not seeking a job, an individual may automatically assume that you *are* and not wish to deal with you. They don't realistically accept that you "just want to shake their hand and become acquainted."

I don't know how many times I called someone, and upon telling them that I was interested in seeking their professional advice, becoming acquainted and gathering some information, I would hear them respond: "Well, we don't have any positions open right now. Just send me your resume and we'll call you."

Yes, it sounds insensitive. It really frustrated me, and you may hear it from time to time. Don't be disheartened. Keep on searching.

To be honest, the most considerate people—those like the woman in the second phone conversation—were individuals who had once stood in unemployment lines themselves. You can be reassured that there are a lot of those people out there who now have jobs, and many will be happy to meet with you and give you some advice.

Here are some hints when calling a total stranger for an informational interview:

1) *Have a connection.* A common acquaintance is best, someone who doesn't mind your using his or her name. Belonging to or involvement in a common organization or activity can also be effective.

2) *Respect the person's time.* Don't forget: just because a person picks up the phone doesn't mean he or she has time to talk. Any time I call *anyone*, the very first words out of my mouth are: "Do you have a minute?" People will appreciate it when you offer first to call back at a more convenient time, because you have caught them at a difficult moment. If you are allowed to continue, get to the point of your call and don't start telling the person your life story.

3) *Make it clear you are not seeking a job interview.* Again, this is sometimes the toughest thing to get through to a person. It is also among the most important.

4) *Tell the person you would like his or her advice.* It flatters people to be sought out for advice. You may actually get some very helpful tips!

5) *Agree to meet at the person's convenience.* This comes back to respecting another person's time. You want to *make the meeting as easy as possible* for him or her.

Key Objectives for the Informational Interview

There is a sort of "bottom line agenda" when going on these types of interviews: *to get the person you are meeting with to know you and find out who they know and to gather information which will be valuable to your eventual search for an employer or customers.*

That really is why you are at the meeting. You want to meet as many people as possible. You want to get your name out and keep it in front of people. You want to gather information. It's that simple.

Some info-interviews can go smoothly; others can be stale and uncomfortable. It depends upon the person with whom you are meeting and your ability to build a rapport with that individual.

First Priority: Make a Good Impression

I'll tell you a secret that a career counselor told me when I was unemployed. This woman had worked with many managers and interviewers, and she pointed out one important tactic.

A manager she knew, while he was talking with an interviewee, always had his secretary lay a rolled up piece of paper on the floor right outside his door. It would always be placed so there was no way anyone coming out of the manager's office would miss it.

The test: whether or not the applicant would pick it up, or leave it for someone else?

The real, implicit question he wanted answered was, does this individual who wishes to work for us really take responsibility? Think about it: what would you do?

That story really hit me hard. Its point is so subtle. Yet that kind of unconscious response says a lot about how we view ourselves and the limits of our responsibility to those around us.

Now, each time I see a piece of litter on the sidewalk, I pick it up. Adopting good observation and listening habits and attitudes can help you make a good first impression. This is probably just as important as knowing how to dress, speak and conduct yourself.

A Secret to Finding Common Ground

When learning about the person you are talking to, seek out something the two of you might have in common. Do you have any other acquaintances you both know? Perhaps you might belong to the same groups or enjoy the same activities and hobbies?

I'll let you in on another secret. Not only in my efforts as a networker, but in the work I have done in fund-raising as well, in which I occasionally meet with influential business leaders, there is one single practice which I have adopted over the last twelve years that has repeatedly allowed me to have something in common with a significant number of people I meet.

I am a National Public Radio listener.

I have found that many (and I would bet most) people in the top positions in this country are avid NPR listeners. National Public Radio news stories are broad based and in depth. Having listened loyally for many years, I know that my horizons have been expanded. I think everyone should listen to NPR for the same reason colleges stress a liberal arts background: you get exposure to a wide variety of topics, *and the expanded knowledge you gain stays with you.*

I'll give you a perfect example. One morning, I drove across town to meet with the president of a large social-service organization in a nearby city. Along the way, I turned on the radio and heard an in-depth NPR report about how so many of the latest *New York Times* bestseller books were those dealing with faith and spirituality.

The man with whom I was about to meet was the president of a YMCA, an organization which regards serving the spiritual needs of individuals as a significant part of its mission. Well, when I sat down to meet with the president, the initial conversation was rather dry and I didn't feel like he was really opening up to me. Then we started talking about the significance of spirituality. When I mentioned the NPR report, suddenly we had something in common! He had heard it too!

That single element really helped me to generate a better rapport, which added to the productivity of the meeting.

If you tend to keep your radio set at just music, try switching to an NPR station, especially in the morning and during afternoon rush hour. You may find that the information you hear today can do wonders for conversation starters tomorrow, next week, or even six months from now.

Learn About the Individual
Who Interviews You and What This Person Does

While in the meeting, you want to learn as much about the individual and the company as possible. Of course, it often helps to know something about the individual and their organization or business before you get to the meeting.

It is important to develop a good understanding of what your new contact does, because it can help you stay in touch with that person, and even better, help you to build a relationship with that contact.

For example, if you come across an article which might pertain to this person's needs, you can cut it out and send it. This reinforcement of the fact that you were listening and sensitive to the needs of your interviewer is much more relevant than sending a holiday greeting card.

Or in another example, suppose you meet with someone who is involved in insurance consulting and estate planning. That person may not have a direct need for you at this time, and you may not really be concerned with planning your estate. (You need to create it first!)

However, over time you may meet another person who could use an estate planner's services. Putting these two people in touch with one another surely would be a good way of establishing a relationship with not just one, but two people! And both of these people will be much more inclined now to do you a favor in return.

Gather as Much Useful Information as Possible

Gather any information which you think may prove useful in helping you jump-start or build your career. It can be information about what is happening in your interviewer's company, the general industry or your community.

The person may privately reveal that while there are no opportunities at his or her company today, certain changes are going to take place over the next several months which may create some opportunities.

This does and can happen, but only after that individual becomes acquainted and is sincerely impressed with you. She would certainly not keep in mind a non-impressive person who appears to care little about the company and just steps into her office to find a job.

Your interviewer may also know what is going on in other companies and around the industry, based upon what she hears from friends and colleagues, not to mention what she reads in a local business publication. You don't know who in the future will prove helpful to you and who won't. So even if the immediate prospects seem bleak, be attentive and sensitive to your contact.

Other Important Tips

One of the first things I did when setting foot in someone's office was to thank him for his time. I understood that the person was busy with schedules to keep and bosses to please. It sincerely meant a lot to me that he would take a few moments out just to chat.

Be sure to point out that you are not directly seeking a job from that person. On the other hand, make no secret of the fact that you are eager to learn about any new opportunity to work in his field in any capacity, either full-time or part-time or on a contract basis. Just make it clear that there is no implied obligation by having this meeting.

While in the meeting, you want to learn as much about the individual and his company as possible. *Don't just sit down and start talking about yourself, which can be a bad habit.* Wait until asked.

Ask questions about the company (specifics that you couldn't learn from some modest research before the meeting) and about what the company's needs are. This is a great way to practice effective listening skills and could give you some ideas for where you can fit into the industry.

Getting Names

One of the most productive ways to start building your contact list is to ask someone you know. Unfortunately, not everyone understands that this is at the heart of building contacts.

I met with many people who appeared, in my own words, dead-end contact meetings.

They were the end of that road as far as obtaining any names was concerned. They either didn't understand that I was looking for names, or they didn't feel comfortable passing out contacts to someone, who in some cases, they had just met.

I'm sure both reasons were true on occasion. I mean, let's face it. What am I really doing when I give a complete stranger a friend's name and tell them to use me as a reference?

I am putting my reputation on the line!

What happens if my friend hires this person, who then turns out to be unreliable and untrustworthy? How does that make me look?

That can be a difficult situation to be in. I have to admit, I have met people whom I would not want using my name as a reference when calling upon a friend, associate or colleague. And I am generally a pretty trusting fellow.

Some people are more trusting than others. **Not everyone you meet is necessarily going to feel comfortable putting you in touch with everyone they know. You shouldn't expect them to.** After all, the two of you just met. Sure, the contact may have your resume or biographical sketch. He might even really know the person who gave you his name. Still, there is something missing: a deeper familiarity, an element of trust, a relationship.

Building Relationships: Simple But Not Easy

Building relationships is the deeper side to networking, and it can be difficult. But building relationships can also be better for you in the long-run. Here's why this is true:

Relationships Are Ongoing and More Sincere

You have some kind of continuing contact or involvement with a person with whom you have a relationship. It doesn't mean you see them or talk to them every day or necessarily every week. Your association, however, is ongoing, reaching beyond a first-time meeting in their office.

You may have heard an expression: "When you meet someone, find a way to stay in touch with them!"

I believe it is true and very important to stay in touch with people. The "how" is most difficult. I didn't feel right calling a person up on the phone or sending them a note, just to find out "how he or she was doing."

In that painful time when I was unemployed, I was more concerned about putting food on the table and really only cared about what the person could *do for me to help me accomplish this necessity*. I am not at all proud of that admission, but it is the truth. I am sure, however, that few people looking for a job will deny this is how they truly feel, whether they are hitting the pavement fresh out of college or have been let go from a previous job. It's our survivalist instinct.

In reality, a note sent out which read:

Just touching base and saying hello. I hope your business is doing fine.
Really meant:
Just letting you know I am still seeking work. Any new leads yet?

Of course, there is nothing wrong with stating the truth in a tactful manner. In fact, the reader might respect your honesty. That doesn't make this kind of note any easier to write. I also don't like reaching out to another person when all I am trying to do is help myself.

It just isn't very sincere. And a lack of sincerity indicates a character flaw on my part and lack of respect for the reader.

Carry Through

Through ongoing interaction and involvement, people know who you are. They are aware of your strengths and weaknesses, which is not bad. They understand what's important to you, not from what you tell them through your words, but through your actions. They have an understanding of the depth of your character. Hopefully, they trust you.

These are things which take time to develop. Once you have this kind of relationship, people usually want to and do give you good references.

For example, let's look at what happened to my good friend, David Glover.

David is an upper level executive with a local utility company, who works in the accounting department. Months ago, he had a brief meeting with Jeff, a college student interested in accounting and its role in business. Jeff had gotten Glover's name from one of David's former colleagues at the utility company.

Jeff was nice and polite. His resume looked good. But, David just didn't see much drive in him and hadn't really heard much from him beyond a follow-up letter. David wasn't even sure if Jeff contacted the two people whose names David reluctantly gave him.

David also attends a local church in which he is fairly active. There, he became acquainted with Susan, who is also a college student majoring in accounting. David knows Susan pretty well. David's wife and Susan's mother are pretty good friends. Susan was a big help to David when the church took on an important mission project. She helped round up other church members her age and younger to take part in the project. Due to Susan's involvement and hard work, this campaign yielded great success and helped a lot of people.

Recently, David learned of a small, local business that needs someone to help keep their books. It would be a part-time job, but could lead to better opportunities. He was asked if he knew of someone who might be qualified and interested.

Who do you think he recommended? Susan or what's-his-name?

Get my point?

It doesn't even matter that David has never worked with Susan on anything related to accounting. *He knows Susan*, the person who gives her time and talents to their church and to serve others. *Jeff*, on the other hand, is that paper resume hidden in a file drawer at work.

Networking Through Career Fairs

Career fairs continue to be an effective means for linking graduating college students with potential employers. For the companies, it is a tremendous means of sampling the talent that is soon to be available to them. For the students, it is a great way to learn of new opportunities, and to network.

These objectives are important, but I suggest an additional goal. It's one thing to sit down with someone for twenty minutes and talk about yourself and what you want to do. But chances are, even at a career fair, that person doesn't care. Her only concern is what you can do for her company.

It is very likely that at a career fair, you will sit down with a recruiter who will invite you to talk about yourself. By all means, do so, and allow the other person to control the conversation. However, he or she will only be hearing what you have to say from the perspective of how you can benefit the company he/she represents. That is why if it is your interest to initiate some kind of relationship, you must also invite the recruiter to tell you about their business. What kind of people does the company hope to add to its team in the future? How does the recruiter see the future of the company?

By asking the recruiter about his or her company, you are actually inquiring about his or her needs.

In the new century, employment isn't about filling jobs...it's about serving needs. Employers attend career fairs for one reason: they need people. It's that simple. You will gain a stronger connection with the people you meet in career fairs and as you network if you practice one simple habit: listening!

It is often said that humans were given two ears and one mouth for a reason. We should each spend at least twice as much time listening to others as we talk.

A Simple Habit To Make Someone's Day— And To Be Remembered

You cannot be everyone's pal. However, your best references are those who can vouch for your character, based upon their relationship with you.

So can we assume that a "contact" you might make through a single brief meeting will be unable to vouch for your character?

Not necessarily so.

Most career counselors recommend "follow-up" letters following any formal meeting. I suppose that's a good habit. The only problem is that most people you formally meet with *expect* to get them. So to be quite honest, they don't do you much good.

In other words, they can hurt you if you don't send them. But they really don't help you if you do. Such is life.

When follow-up notes really make an impact is when they aren't expected. Have you ever been in a position when a receptionist or someone has greatly helped you out by just doing their job?

While researching this book, I was trying to find some statistics but ran into some trouble. Then I came across a local organization which collected the same data I needed for a project of their own. I spoke with a lady named Karen on the phone, who offered to photocopy the materials—thirty-plus pages—and mail them to me.

From my perspective, she was under no obligation to even give me the time of day. Yet Karen took the time to help me anyway. Better still, the information was exactly what I was looking for.

As far as she was concerned, she was just doing her job. But from my point of view, she saved me several hours of digging at the library and probably a couple dollars' worth of copying. To me, it was a big favor.

I decided to let her know a few months later by dropping her a thank you note. I wrote a short memo saying how much her service helped me and that I appreciated it. I presume she received it quite unexpectedly. I hope it improved her day and that maybe she kept it. I am also more confident that if I ever call on her again—within a reasonable amount of time—she will remember who I am, even though we have never met face to face.

I am certainly not the first to stress the importance of follow-up or thank you notes, but think of it this way. Suppose you are having a dreary day, and perhaps not feeling so good about yourself. Then you receive a small note in the mail, one that says that you are appreciated and that you do a good job. Now, how would you feel after someone took the time to write you a note, thanking you for your help?

Wouldn't you like to give someone else that feeling, especially if they were helpful to you in some way? And wouldn't you like to turn a casual acquaintance into a good friend? Then do it. Don't wait!

Building Contacts and Building Relationships:
The Fundamental Differences

Let's quickly review the main differences between building contacts and building relationships.

BUILDING CONTACTS...
...is short term in nature.

It usually focuses on trying to meet as many people in the shortest amount of time. If a person you meet does not have an immediate need for your services and cannot lead you to anyone else, then there is little foundation for a long-term relationship.

...emphasizes quantity.

The more names you collect, the deeper your network of contacts becomes.

...is based upon the age-old premise of "It's not what you know but who you know."

This combines with the previous premise of collecting as many names as possible. You must have as many acquaintances as you can to ensure that the right opportunity will come through at the right time.

BUILDING RELATIONSHIPS...

...is long term in nature.

When jump-starting your career, you are taking active steps to prepare for the future. The people you meet and develop bonds with will hopefully be with you for **the rest of your life**, regardless of the nature of those relationships.

Thinking long-term goes way past the day after graduation. You are forming relationships with people whom you want to stay in touch with long after you graduate.

...emphasizes quality.

You can't form deep relationships with every person with whom you come in contact. That should be, though, an underlying goal. Keeping this in mind will help you notice opportunities to form those relationships beyond the acquaintance stage.

...dispels the "who you know" attitude.

In reality, it is not just "who you know." Most often it is the following three elements:

- Who you are (your integrity)...
- What you know and can do (your qualifications)...
- And how well another individual knows you (your relationships)...which can get you through the door and keep you there.

What Next? Here Are Some Steps You Can Take Today

1) Before you start informational interviewing, begin with generating a list of everyone you know. You can divide the people up into several categories, based upon the nature of your relationship with them. This can include family, friends, work,

community (such as church or volunteer work), school and other associations.

2) When you are calling to set up informational interviews, it is helpful to have some kind of script in hand, so you are sure of what you want to say. It doesn't have to be long, and there is no real set way to do it. Just remember to clearly state that you are calling as part of your own personal research and to seek the person's professional advice.

3) Pick out the person on your list with whom you feel most comfortable and set up an informational interview! Get started in the process. As you meet with others, find out from them what they have done and what secrets they may be able to offer that will enable you to meet and get to know others.

4) Start paying closer attention to the local news and listening to NPR. Not only can the news be helpful in carrying on conversations, you never know when you may hear or read something that could prove helpful or interesting to one of your interviewees.

5) Take steps to strengthen your relationships with other people, to take them beyond handshakes and common acquaintance-ship. If you find someone you meet to be helpful and you seem to hit it off, look into forming a mentor-protege relationship with that person. Maybe you can also begin a volunteering or start an internship position.

6) Do the unexpected. In this chapter we spoke about the possibilities of sending notes and making another person's day better. As you meet with different people, *listen* to each one of them. Find out what the person's concerns are, what problems he or she needs solved. *Listen for your opportunity to fill his or her need.* When you find the opportunity, act upon it with discretion and spontaneity. Meet that person once in her office, and she might remember who you are. Solve her problem, and she *will* remember you!

6

Start Building Your Network

"It was having a common acquaintance who knew both myself and the hiring manager that gave me an edge in filling a recently opened position."
- Laura Loescher
Hampshire College
Economics

While an undergraduate at Hampshire College, Laura Loescher invested her time in internships and service activities with a variety of organizations. These positions helped her to focus her interest in social justice and political activism, and to begin building relationships with other people. "I felt that these service internships would help me get a better idea of where my strengths were," Laura comments.

Laura's public service training and her rigorous undergraduate course work in economics and social science helped her develop many strong qualifications. Laura says that, "The relationships I developed as a direct result of my service work opened some doors for me when I moved to San Francisco. I knocked on the door of a firm which manages six socially responsible mutual funds. And it was having a common acquaintance who knew both myself and the hiring manager that gave me an edge in filling a recently opened position."

This edge enabled Laura to obtain a job researching companies that are interested in being added to investment portfolios. She determines where these companies stand on such issues as nuclear power, employee relations, the environment and product quality. Laura also examines the companies' diversity in the work place, on their board of directors and within their management.

Laura's advice: "Where I work, I see more students on informational interviews than on job interviews. The students are much more likely to get in to see someone if they have a strong connection, not just with an acquaintance, but with someone they truly know."

"Getting a job is definitely a combination of experience and relationships," Laura continues. "You have to work at building both, and I feel that service work and internships are an ideal way to do just that. It's a great way to network."

So far, I have discussed some key issues regarding networking. From Laura's words here, and from Adam's story in the previous chapter, you can now understand the importance of building relationships in order to jump-start your career. You have also learned that networking means not viewing others merely as resources that enable you to get ahead, but as individuals who have responsibilities, feelings and needs which you can aid them in fulfilling.

Networking should be a regular activity as you move through your college career. At first, the process can seem daunting, but as you become more experienced you will become more adept at it. By now you may be asking another key question:

"*How* Do I Start?"

If you want to build a strong, integrated network of contacts and friends so you can begin the process of jump-starting your career while still in school, the time to start is now.

It may sound overwhelming. However, remember your objective. You aren't out to build the longest list in networking history.

Some of what I am going to say next overlaps with some points you may have read elsewhere in this book. In fact, I want to reiterate some of them, because they are extremely important for you to remember.

1. *Volunteer.*

Remember what you read earlier about the benefits of volunteering? *Volunteering is one of the most effective ways to build relationships with people.*

It runs much deeper than the informational interview. Your involvement with an organization bonds you to other members or volunteers with that same organization. By working together to reach a common goal, you automatically build relationships.

That doesn't mean you have to hang out with these people every weekend, or even see them on a weekly basis. If you have the opportunity to connect with these other individuals regularly, which volunteering allows you to do, then you automatically let them know you better. They discover your talents, your values and your character. You in turn discover theirs. These are things which cannot normally be accomplished through a single thirty-minute meeting.

Before you start getting involved with one of them, just remember to focus on something that interests you. Make sure that it involves work and activities that you enjoy.

If your heart isn't really into something, then it will show in the quality of your work and in how you relate to people. That will reflect badly upon you and do much more harm than good.

Remember, wherever there are opportunities to serve, there are friends to be made.

Not superficial acquaintances.

Not just names to jot down.

Not temporary contacts...*but friends*. They are all around us.

2. *Become an intern.*

Many national and local organizations, especially in the non-profit and communications areas, have intern programs. There are lots of new books, among them *Peterson's Guide to Interning*, which detail thousands of these opportunities. I will discuss internships in more detail in chapter 8.

3. Get a part-time job.

Sounds obvious, doesn't it? By taking on a part-time job at a company that employs the kind of professional you want to become, how can that not help you?

When I was in college, I worked for a while as a law clerk. Now I was not studying to be an attorney, but many clerks I met there were. This job paid about the same as a job flipping burgers, but the other rewards were working in an environment that they were planning to spend most of their careers in and connecting with existing attorneys. It was also the perfect chance simply to get to know some people outside the college environment.

4. Adopt a mentor.

Perhaps the advice should read: *Have a mentor adopt you.* A mentor is usually a professional person at a top-level within an organization who counsels, advises and guides a less experienced individual.[1] A mentor can be great if you have a fairly clear idea of what you want to do for a living, or are at least considering. By associating closely with someone already out in the field, you can learn all kinds of insights that you won't get in the classroom.

A mentor can even help you be sure you are making the right decision.

- You can observe the person "in action" in the courtroom, meeting room, office, or wherever he or she works.
- You can learn how he or she came to be in the position. You'll hear about the pitfalls as well as the victories. Don't be surprised when a mentor tells you he or she started out in a completely different direction.
- You can learn of different types of positions in the mentor's field, because the person may have held most of them on his or her way up the ladder.

- You can gain a clearer career direction for yourself, from the mentor's guidance in academic choices and outside activities.
- From your mentor's connections with other people, he or she may be able to help you find new opportunities to serve and learn.

No matter where you are in your career, it is always good to have a mentor. This is especially important in college when you are at a critical stage in your personal development.

For example, a mentorship program in Chicago geared towards minorities has many students working side-by-side with their mentors. The experience of bonding with another professional, getting into a different physical environment and receiving one-on-one guidance has proved pivotal for many students who would otherwise not be encouraged to pursue higher education, much less professional careers.[2]

When seeking a mentor or mentors, you will want to look for individuals who:

- *Inspire genuine respect and for whom you feel a level of trust.*

Just because a professional colleague works in your future field and has achieved a level of success which you wish to attain doesn't automatically qualify the person to be your mentor.

While all people deserve our respect as human beings, let's face reality. We respect some people more than others. People may be professionally and financially successful, but are they honest? How did they get where they are?

Joseph, a law student I knew, began a mentor-protege relationship with the attorney for whom he was working as a clerk. Joseph was excited and thought it was a great match—until he began to notice very subtle signs of dishonesty in the way this attorney went about his business, as well as in his personal life. How a person conducts himself in all roles *makes a difference*. In the words of Gandhi: "Life is one indivisible whole."[3]

Now I am not encouraging you to judge other people. In this case, as in Joseph's case, you must follow your heart. When you are evaluating a person who may have a significant role in your life, you must respect that individual or you will not respect his or her counsel. Seriously consider this quality when searching for a mentor.

- *Display character traits, abilities and values similar to your own.*

This doesn't mean you must agree on everything or do everything alike. But whether or not the person possesses qualities you admire helps to determine whether your prospective mentor makes a good *role model* for you.

As we have already discussed, volunteer service and internships are also great ways to meet people who share similar values to your own and have reached admirable heights. You may also seek out mentors in your university, professional clubs and organizations (more on these later) and part-time employment.

- *Can connect you with other significant people and meaningful opportunities.*

This is not a prerequisite, but it certainly can make a difference in your future. Chances are, your mentor will be able to provide you with guidance and leads through his or her own network of clients, colleagues and friends. As your relationship with your mentor strengthens, you will most likely be introduced to or come across these people naturally.

- ***Could use your*** *help on some level in return for his or her guidance and advice.*

Remember the big picture: the process of jump-starting your career includes serving the needs of others. Why should your mentor be different? There are probably many ways in which you can make your mentor relationship reciprocal.
    - A law student can do research and perform clerical functions, not to mention assisting with the needs of clients.
    - An accounting major can perform bookkeeping tasks.
    - A student majoring in communications can help write and proof copy, as well as many other marketing/PR functions.

- An education major can certainly be useful helping out in and outside the classroom. Ask any teacher!

Remember, it is not only what others can do for you. What can you do for them?

Many professional people are very willing to become mentors once someone asks them. They often see it as a chance to help a younger person and to give back to a profession that has done very well for them. The trick is finding one yourself if your college doesn't have a structured mentoring program. If it doesn't, here's what you can do:

- Check your career-guidance office and ask about finding a mentor. A counselor should be able to give you some leads.
- Call some local chapters of the professional organizations for your chosen field. An official there may also be able to mention it at the next meeting (don't be surprised if he or she invites you) or even run a blurb in the newsletter. While you have the person on the phone, remember to ask about volunteer and intern opportunities!
- Consider looking to those in your present environment like a college teacher or professor.

Building Relationships with Your Professors

You may recall from the introduction that my first job opportunity came from conversations with a journalism professor at Ohio State. I had many questions about the subject she was teaching and found myself going to see her on several occasions. At one meeting, she casually gave me a name and a telephone number which she mentioned was a possible job lead. In fact I got the job. For me, it was my very first full-time professional job, which enabled me to build a wealth of new skills which I will always carry with me.

Many teachers stay in touch with their students long after school is over. Several years ago, an article in *Business Week*[4] cited the case of a group of MBAs who started their own businesses, but were not using the typical mentors they could have found had they worked at large companies. Instead, many of these MBAs stayed in contact with their professors for years after graduation, using them as advisers while their start-up enterprises grew.

When I was a design student at an art college, many teachers there had outside business practices, such as consulting and freelancing. There was one industrial design teacher in particular who spent a lot of his off-duty time giving out-of-classroom guidance *and work experience* to several students, including some roommates of mine.

However, he didn't go around announcing this extra perk to the class. In fact, he was very discreet about his choices. The students had to come to him—*on their own.*

The fact is that many professors you have right now can be invaluable sources of advice, guidance and networking. Teachers and professors have associations and relationships in the business world as well as the campus community.

When you come across a teacher whom you feel might make a positive mentor or role model for you, here are some steps you may take to make that relationship a reality:

1) *Take as many of their classes as you can.*

This is assuming that the courses are in line with your field of study, although that is not a requirement.

As you attend class and take notes, reveal your genuine interest. Be visible. Ask questions. Be enthusiastic. Communicate.

Imagine how you would feel as a committed teacher when you see the sparks of enthusiasm and learning in a student. **Get the teacher excited about helping you!**

2) *Make time after class for further discussion and to begin getting acquainted.*

You may notice that rarely are the best instructors standing at the head of the classroom alone upon dismissal. There is normally a group of students who stampede the podium, ready to ask several questions for further discussion and explanation.

You may also notice each day that the group is comprised of roughly the same students! This doesn't mean you can't join in also to ask some questions. Don't be timid. Give it a try.

3) *Visit the teacher during his or her office hours to seek further advice on setting and reaching your career goals.*

You'll flatter and honor your teacher by seeking him or her out after class. On a regular basis, see your teacher during set office hours. Share with him or her your plans and goals. Ask about his or her experiences. Seek the teacher's advice.

Get to know your instructors and let them get to know you. This way, you are not simply a nameless face in the crowd.

4) *Allow the relationship to grow naturally.*

It is always important to respect other people's time. You are not intruding as long as you use office hours and keep appointments. The teacher is there to help you. That's part of the reason a teacher went into education: to make a difference and bring knowledge and guidance to young people.

Develop the relationship gradually. Don't push it too much. Before you know it, if all goes well, your teacher will anticipate your questions and your visits. Best of all, your teacher will get to know you as a person. Businesses and organizations turn to college professors all the time for help (more on that later).

Remember the example in chapter 5 of David Glover? He is the accounting executive who, upon learning of a job opening, didn't choose Jeff, the young man whom he met once in an informational interview, but did select Susan, the young woman who attends and participates at his church. Without hesitation, he passed a job lead onto the person he already knew.

Similarly with your teacher, you have a choice. You can decide to remain an anonymous, faceless body sitting in a weekly lecture. Or you can become a participant whom that teacher knows and cares about. Then, when your professor sees or learns of opportunities, that professor will want to pass them along to you. The teacher will write letters of recommendation for you. He or she will put you in touch with people who may help you.

When a teacher advises you and guides you, and listens and shares in your hopes and dreams as well as your frustrations, that teacher will have a greater ownership in your career. On a subconscious level, your instructor will care more about seeing you succeed. Why?

Because your success will also be the teacher's success.

Other Campus Opportunities to Build Relationships
Advisors

Finishing my degree at a large university, I had literally no relationship with my "assigned" academic advisor who was a faculty member within the department of my major. However, that was probably more my fault than anyone else's. I never went out of my way to set up an appointment. I never called on the advisor. I certainly could not expect that person to call me—he was busy enough as it was.

If you meet and do not feel a match between yourself and your assigned academic advisor, then by all means find another mentor. However, your assigned academic advisor can be a great person to start with, especially if you feel anxiety about approaching someone else.

Professional Student Organizations

Many professional and volunteer organizations have student chapters, especially on our nation's larger college campuses. If no student chapters exist on yours, you can usually apply for a student membership in a professional organization at a reduced rate, and thus attend their meetings normally held off-campus. What an opportunity to meet influential people!

To really benefit from these organizations you should apply the same principles which you apply to volunteering. Beyond doing a good deed, your objectives are to meet people who have the same or similar interests, and to get others to know you.

To gain valuable experience developing skills and working with people, you must put your heart and effort into it. To merely attend meetings and not participate is a complete waste of time. Even worse, to commit half-heartedly and produce poor results can damage your reputation and your future career. Enthusiasm and effort are necessary if you are to profit.

For a sampling of these professional organizations, refer to appendix I. For a more comprehensive list, check out the *Encyclopedia of Associations*. Most colleges and public libraries have copies on hand, and local editions are published in many communities. The yellow pages of your phone directory should also have a section called, "Associations, Professional," or a similar listing.

Study Groups

In my work, I recently had the opportunity to meet with a surgeon who practices in a large teaching hospital in a nearby city. This is an institution which, as a community hospital, has long sponsored new medical school graduates for their residency training. Medical education, they boasted, was a key factor in maintaining top quality health care for the people of the community.

"To me and to many others, clinical practice alone is not enough," said this highly respected physician. "The daily interaction with young doctors challenges you and keeps your days lively and different. Also, the ongoing process of teaching, learning and sharing reinforces our own knowledge of—and enthusiasm for—this fascinating practice of medicine! As professionals, we are all lifetime students."

This summarizes the benefits of working with study groups not only to the student, but to teachers as well. Clearly, these benefits are twofold: study groups reinforce your own knowledge, and they also allow you to meet other people and form relationships.

A way to apply this strategy on campus is to organize study groups for your classes.

Look at it this way. Have you ever found yourself in the position of explaining a situation or dilemma to another person? Didn't you then, *after mentally processing and then communicating the information to another*, have a much stronger understanding of the information yourself? This is a good way for learning to occur.

That's what the doctor meant when he said that education—for the teacher as well as for the student—reinforces and challenges his or her own knowledge and skills.

The other benefit, of course, is the potential for building relationships and working in groups. While most of the topics we have discussed in this book concern meeting with people in your own community and on campus, don't overlook your colleagues. Those other students sitting next to you in class may be your passport not only to friendship but to future career opportunities.

Some of your best relationships may come out of your years in college. I know some of mine did. And it isn't just teachers and administrators from whom you can benefit. In fact, just because those people sitting next to you are also in school does not mean that you cannot learn from them. They, in turn, can learn much from you.

Roughly *half* of our country's college student population falls under the traditional age category. The rest are regarded as *non-traditional*—individuals in their thirties and forties with years of experience already behind them. Do you know what that means?

It means that, chances are, the person sitting next to you in class has already worked in the real world. On average, that person carries with him or her ten years of career experience. That person probably has new perspectives to bring to a study group, as well as possible contacts. Take advantage of the multi-dimensional makeup of many college classes. Listen, communicate and form new relationships.

Beyond the Campus: Who Else Do You Know?

You may start getting tired of hearing this question. However, it must be continually asked. Each semester you are in college you will have different professors and classmates. Your campus environment may be a good place to start, but you must move on.

So, who else do you know? Again, revise your list on a yearly basis. Through your intimates and family members you probably already have a strong network in place.

Some of the more typical entries on your list:

- Your immediate family members (parents, siblings, grandparents)
- Your extended family members (uncles, aunts, cousins)
- Previous teachers (both high school and college)
- Former bosses from past jobs

- Your landlord
- Your insurance agent (or any other professional, such as lawyer, accountant, etc.)
- Salespeople, beauticians and barbers
- Your minister or rabbi
- Other members of your religious congregation
- Your banker
- Others with whom you volunteer or serve your community
- Former classmates from high school
- Former college classmates who have graduated
- Fellow members in your professional association

So what do you think? Possible network? Not a bad start? The only problem is that it is "asleep." That is, most of the people in your network may not necessarily see you in terms of the career for which you are preparing. Instead, you are to them whatever is the nature of your relationship: the niece or nephew, the client, the patient, the fellow club member, the person next door.

If you have a network that is "asleep," what you must do now is "wake 'em up!"

In other words, you want those around you to be aware of all you can do—of what kind of services you hope to provide for them and other people as you build your career.

There are many ways to do this. Your value depends on several factors, which includes the nature of your relationship with each person, what his or her specific needs are and the services you can provide.

In my opinion, no matter how well someone knows you personally, it is always better to *demonstrate* to another what you can do and have them *benefit* from it. Most people, whether they are neighbors, uncles and aunts or fellow church members, will have a much stronger opinion of your professional abilities if they have benefited from them, rather than being told about the benefits you could provide.

Imagine your uncle owns a dry-cleaning business. You're a student majoring in business or marketing or accounting—take your pick. Now, in the interest of building your network, you want to contact him to let him know what goals you are pursuing.

There are two possible approaches. One can be to set up a meeting, where you might just sit and talk and perhaps ask some advice. You might even pass on a copy of your resume for him to keep on hand. Of course, you also want to know if he has any contacts that you may call upon.

The second approach can be different. Instead of calling on your uncle and asking for advice and some names, you ask your uncle *about his business*. Many scenarios can be imagined. For instance, you probably wouldn't have known without asking him that he was seeing a portion of his business slip away because of some new competition. Or perhaps he has been trying to upgrade and increase the efficiency of his bookkeeping operation but just can't seem to take the time to learn how to operate a computer.

By asking about his business, you are actually *inquiring about his needs*.

In response, you can lend your talents to examining the marketplace, the competition and the industry. Perhaps you could even help him draw up a new marketing plan that helps him increase his business, despite the competition.

Or maybe you know, like the back of your hand, the very software and systems about which he is pulling his hair out. You help him choose a computer and software, and you dedicate one afternoon per week for the next four months to getting his books totally converted and up to speed. In addition, you give him the very lessons he needs to eventually run the system himself. You even uncover some opportunities for him to save on his taxes and increase efficiency.

Now what do you think will be his view of you?

He will definitely be impressed. He will be sold on, not to mention indebted to your abilities. But what kind of connections does a person who operates a dry-cleaning business have that can help you? The answer is hanging on those racks in the back of the store. What do you see?

Men's suits. Women's suits. Odds are, your uncle has some pretty influential people walking through his doors each week. If he is a good businessman, he knows many of them by name. After you have helped his business, how enthusiastic do you think he will feel about touting your name to them? A lot more so than if all you did was hand him your resume and walk out while he remained preoccupied with his own troubles.

You may read this example and murmur, "That is so hypothetical. How can it relate to me?" Sure, it's a fabricated story. But the principles apply everywhere.

As you network, you search for needs. You provide for needs. You benefit people. You build relationships. Then, when opportunities arise, you get rewarded.

What Next? Here Are Some Steps You Can Take Today

1) Seek out someone you admire and consider "adopting" the person as a mentor or role model. Seek the person's advice and learn from his or her experience. Don't view the relationship as a one-way deal. If this individual is helping you, then you must also seek ways to help that person, in return.

2) When you begin to establish a relationship with another person, look into spending a day with him or her. Learn about his or her environment and daily life.

3) Utilize the wisdom and experience of your teachers. Allow your teachers to build a sense of *ownership* in your success. Of the classes you are currently taking, which instructor do you find the most interesting? Enlist the teacher's guidance.

4) Become involved in a professional organization, either on campus or within your community. Again, go into it with the resolve to make a *contribution*. Commit yourself to having some impact and allowing others to get to know you.

5) If the idea of forming a study group sounds helpful, why not take it a step further? *Form a career-building support group.* In it, you and your peers can come from many career backgrounds.

You can lend support to each other and share your experiences. Problems can be discussed. Brainstorming will provide a variety of suggestions. A helpful tip one person gets in an interview can be shared to benefit the group.

Regular gatherings can also help keep you on your toes and working, if you suggest that for each meeting you have to develop some new stories to tell or have some new information to share.

6) Wake up your existing network! Let your family and friends know you are ready to seek job opportunities. Find out ways you can use your knowledge to their benefit.

Small Companies, Big Opportunities

A few years ago I wrote my first book, *Advertise! An Assessment of Fundamentals for Small Business*. In the introduction, I recalled my first real-world work experience in the area of marketing communications:

During my early years of college, I took a summer job with a small pizza shop in my hometown of Pittsburgh, Pennsylvania. While my job started out as a driver and pie-maker, I did get involved in organizing marketing strategies to boost the business of the store, which was only a few months old.

Since the business was new, there was not a big budget for promotions. One method the owner preferred was rounding up some of the local kids, taking them to some of the other areas to which we wished to expand and having them go from house to house distributing flyer-coupons. The only payment those kids got was free pizzas.

At a cost of barely seventy-five cents per pizza, one might assume it a highly economical promotion. But soon enough, the kids started asking for more than just pizza. (Could you blame them?)

So we sat down to make some decisions, and the budget made them for us. The only advertising which we could afford was in the classified ads.

We utilized a direct mail publication called *The Pennysaver*, and ran a three-by-five inch advertisement with coupons in it. The very day after that first issue with our ad was mailed out, we had a surge of phone calls. In just one month, after some modest investments in the classifieds, we expanded our business threefold.

I relate this experience to you because I want to point something out: I learned more about business working in that little pizza shop than I learned in a classroom, at least at the art college I was attending at the time.

I'm not saying that classroom learning isn't important. It is. However, sometimes the subjects studied impart only abstract theories. Although these help one's general understanding, they do not teach practicalities such as how to provide a benefit to a customer, patient or client through a product or service while earning a profit in the process.

And most seasoned business and professional people will tell you that it takes a lot of common sense and experience to succeed.

All businesses, organizations and professions exist for the same reasons: to serve their clients and customers, and to generate profits for those who provide these services or products. They do not exist to employ people, but they will employ as few or as many people as it takes—be it three or three-thousand—to achieve those objectives.

As you read and consider where you may seek or create opportunities for yourself, remember that point. Business aims to sell a product or service and earn a profit. Non-profit organizations and professional practices also have a service or mission to implement. While non-profit organizations do not claim a "profit" in the sense that businesses do, they still try to have some money left over when the yearly books are closed. This leftover money is referred to as a "surplus," which then gets recycled back into the organization.

Either way, find out what they aim to accomplish. Then ask yourself, how can you help them? Answer this question, and you're halfway home.

What I hope you will learn from this chapter is that there are likely as many opportunities to make yourself useful by working in a small company or business, organization or institution as there are through the larger, well-known corporations.

The challenge is what we have discussed before—being in the right place at the right time. In other words, you have to be lucky. Fortunately, learning to be lucky by learning to be in the right place at the right time is half of what this book is all about.

Just What Is a Small Business or Organization?

When we speak of small business, we are talking about small to medium-sized companies or organizations. In a few cases, less than 500 employees; in many situations, less than 100; and in most, less than twenty.

In the for-profit sector, small businesses make up the majority of the United States economy. That has pretty much been the case for a long time. But now such companies are being recognized as a tremendous source for future job growth.

According to the United States Department of Commerce, more than 90 percent of the 3.5 million new jobs created each year are in firms of four employees or less. In fact, government data reveals that the fastest job growth occurs within companies of less than twenty employees.

These new "microbusinesses"[1] developed in a service-oriented, information economy. They are small and young, and some are highly dependent upon technology. They also tend to have great outreach, from across the state line to across the globe.

Some of them are functioning in the way that many of today's huge corporations aim to: as a small, tightly-knit group of specialized managers working with outside groups (outsizing) to create tangible results.[2]

Why a Small Business Owner—an Entrepreneur— May Be More Likely to Give You a Shot

There will always be competition in the job market, and that's good. Competition keeps you on your toes. But when you go after opportunities in small firms in ways that we will describe, then you will less likely be put in positions where you are competing directly with someone else for the same job.

Why? *The answer is timing.*

In small businesses no one has time for repeated interviews, nor are polished interview answers a requisite. You want to informally make yourself acquainted and available to people—and sooner or later someone will have a need to be filled. These small business owners don't always have time to run a lot of advertisements or scan a horde of resumes. They need someone who can get the job done NOW! Their businesses are at stake!

If they can call you on the phone or call you from the next room, then this is your chance! No resume? Who cares! You have already demonstrated to the person or someone that person knows what you can do. That's all that matters!

This is important, because when you compete for a position or opportunity in the conventional sense at the beginning of your career, very seldom will you have as much experience as a more seasoned candidate. Enthusiasm and proximity, however, can help you seize the opportunity.

Four Distinct Advantages of Working in a Small Business Environment
There Is Less Bureaucracy

Often, in large companies, you are part of a *system*. I remember when I was being interviewed to work for a large software company, I met with two separate individuals that afternoon. The first was a human resources manager, who kept telling me about their strict procedures and corporate policies. She could not stop warning me about how they would double-check my references and background, even after I started working.

Then I met with a person in the communications department, with whom I might be working if I were hired. We had a terrific conversation. We talked about different experiences and work situations and had genuinely great rapport. In the process of discussing the job opening in greater detail, I learned more about the position and realized that I was probably not the best candidate to fill it. But the point was that we talked about the work and its creative dimensions, not company policies.

In fact, I wasn't offered the position; I most likely wouldn't have accepted it if I was. The first person to whom I spoke had strongly affected my assessment of the company, and I wasn't eager to work in such a political, bureaucratic environment.

Large companies are often bureaucracies which stress job titles and company-wide policies over flexibility and individuality. For example, in some large businesses, although you may be very skillful and useful in a function which may not fall under your job description, you could jeopardize your position by trying to serve that function.

Most companies with more than a handful of employees have some form of political dynamics going on. But when it comes to red-tape and bureaucratic waste, most small business managers can't afford them. In a small company, the atmosphere is usually more laid back and you will wear many hats. If you can produce results, then more power to you, whatever your job title. Typically, in small businesses there is also less routine, less procedure. If it means giving a new kid—who's been expressing some helpful suggestions and is always ready to pitch in—a shot at a project, then why the heck not?

There Are Often Greater, More Flexible Opportunities

We know that all of industry is changing in response to new technological innovations and economic realities. Workers must learn to adapt to these changes and learn to take on new responsibilities.

In my first full-time position, I handled all desktop publishing and other marketing communications for a small building products distributor. This meant that I got to wear many hats. I worked as the copywriter, designer, printing buyer, price estimator and occasionally as a customer representative. Overall, it was a great and varied experience.

Because of downsizing, multi-functional positions are also becoming the norm in many larger companies as they reduce their staffs. The more roles you can fill, the better. I still sometimes hear the expression: "Pick one thing and do it better than anyone else." However, doing one thing and one thing alone is becoming less and less appealing to employers in the private, non-profit and public sectors these days.

Small company and organization jobs, like volunteer work, can offer you many opportunities, because they have limited resources and must get as much benefit from every volunteer and employee as they can. If a need arises and you are present, willing and able, then go for it!

You Can Develop Better Relationships

In most small companies, you work in close proximity with everyone on the staff. This will help you really get to know all the people you work with—something very difficult to do at a large company with hundreds of employees. This closeness might also allow you to develop mentor-protege relationships with some of the staff.

You May See Results Much Faster

We define results here in two ways. The first is the tangible benefit you produce from your work efforts—such as the increased sales, the debugged computer, the reduction in office expenses, the new company brochure or increased morale among the employees.

In a larger company, before you can accomplish any of these tasks, you might need to hold off until you have filled out the right paperwork or until the project goes through the chain of command and gets approved. But in a smaller company, where you have daily contact with your boss, you can often get your projects approved quickly and with no fuss of filling out forms or other types of delays. That way, you can immediately tackle a problem or a project, and you can see the results of your work much faster.

The second kind of result comes after the first: your reward. You receive this reward once you have proved your worth by successfully completing your projects.

Since smaller companies have less bureaucracy, significant accomplishments are more likely to be recognized quickly, and this recognition can occur in a variety of ways. You might get a pat on the back, a promotion or a raise. You might even be hired full-time!

Three Ways to Get Your Foot in the Door

Some of these ideas may appear obvious, but just remember this: 95 percent of my suggestions rest upon being in the right place at the right time, not on any convoluted or secret method. *There is no sure-fire path to anything when the decisions of and relationships with people are concerned.* But there are things you can try that often produce results.

Seek an Entry-level Job, Part-time Employment or Volunteer Internship

If you know of a small company, industry, organization or group that you might like to work for professionally, use the informational interview and other techniques you have learned in this book to get your foot in the door. Study what the company's needs are and explain to the interviewer how you can fill them.

You might go directly to the person in charge of employment at the company or in the department where you wish to work. If you are successful in making this connection, then you can offer your services.

The worst that can happen is that they say no. But they might surprise you and say yes!

Other methods to find such opportunities are scanning bulletin boards. Most colleges have employment offices from different companies come to visit their campuses, and bulletin boards are hung up expressly for these companies to post their job opportunities. You might also check bulletin boards at your local library or supermarket for job opportunities.

Another option is going to a temporary employment agency.

Unlike a few years ago when temp agencies filled mostly clerical and manual labor positions, today, many temp firms now are specializing in professional areas like accounting, computers, the law and the health industry because of a change in hiring practices.

The reason for this change is simple. Many employers are reluctant to hire new people for permanent positions. Instead, they prefer to choose from people with whom they already are familiar: their temps, interns and part-timers. An Olsten Corporation survey of human resources executives found that 63 percent of them stated they use temporary services to find permanent employees.[3]

Make sure to tell the agency what kind of job or industry you are interested in. A temp agency wants the person sent to a particular company to be a good fit with the atmosphere and needs of their clients. It makes them look bad if a candidate doesn't quickly fit in. When you work hard and look good, they look good. Therefore, it is in everyone's best interest that you enjoy your job and are satisfied with your position

Yet another option is to look for an internship. I will discuss internships in greater detail in chapter 8. But for now, you should know that internships afford good connections, and the best time to do them is before you graduate. Even if a small company doesn't have a regular job opening, perhaps they can make room for you as an intern. These types of internships might even provide more flexible hours or more varied opportunities than a typical job might offer.

See what is available. Be persistent and professional at all times. You would be surprised at how many successful careers and businesses are launched by someone simply knocking on the door and saying, "May I help?"

If You Are Interested in a Specific Business or Industry, Seek Out the Local Organizations Which Cater to that Industry

I don't think there is a single trade, profession or industry in this country that doesn't have its own local association. Many areas of business, as you may guess, have dozens of such small organizations. As I discussed in chapter 4, most of these organizations are non-profit, and thus often use volunteers and interns.

Be Sure to Ask the People You Know Whom They Know!

This may sound obvious, but don't overlook family members and long-time friends. You can never anticipate whom they may know and introduce you to. They may have friends who are small business owners or small business employees.

Seek Out Entrepreneurs

If you feel you would like to seek out a relationship or an opportunity with an entrepreneur but are at a loss for ideas on where to start, the following suggestions may prove helpful. Bear in mind that, in addition to these suggestions, professional organizations can also be a reliable source for new small business and professional contacts.

Check for a Small Business Incubator in Your Community

A small business incubator is a support center which nurtures small businesses during the critical start-up phase, when they are most vulnerable. Participating enterprises, which must be reviewed and approved much the same way they would be for venture capitalists, operate under a single roof. Incubators rent office space at a reduced cost and provide hands-on management assistance, access to financing and orchestrated exposure to critical business or technical support services.

The primary goal of an incubator is to nurture a business to the point where it becomes financially viable and thus able to "graduate" to free-operating status. This process normally takes two to three years.

According to the National Business Incubation Association (NBIA), a private, not-for-profit 501(c)(3) organization in Athens, Ohio, there are more than 800 incubators operating in North America—up from 12 in 1980.

Some incubators focus on specific industries and some focus more generally, such as on businesses which deal with research or high technology. Other incubators foster service sector businesses and light manufacturing.

Bear in mind that a small business in the incubation stage will not necessarily be the best place to start if you are looking to make a lot of money. It all depends on the enterprise's cash flow and financial strength. Many entrepreneurs and organizers, during the period of starting out, pay themselves very little if anything at all. Instead, they choose to reinvest their earnings back into their businesses.

Before you dismiss this option, think about it. If you are a college student and are going to be working for peanuts anyway, a start-up small business can offer an ideal opportunity. It can also be your chance to enter a successful venture on the ground floor. As the business begins to prosper, so do you!

Incubators are initiated and supported by a wide variety of groups and organizations. Some of the former are funded as non-profits, others are funded by private groups, and still others are funded by colleges and universities. For a place to start, check with your own school and see if it works with a business incubator.

According to NBIA's website (www.nbia.org), the economic contribution of incubators should not go unnoticed:

For every $1 of estimated annual public operating subsidy provided to the incubator, clients and graduates of NBIA member incubators generate approximately $45 in local tax revenue alone.

NBIA members report that 84 percent of incubator graduates stay in their communities and continue to provide a return to their investors.

Publicly supported incubators create jobs at a cost of about $1,100 each, whereas other publicly supported job creation mechanisms commonly cost more than $10,000 per job created.

NBIA estimates that North American incubator clients and graduates have created approximately half a million jobs since 1980. That is enough jobs to employ every person living in Denver, Colorado.

Every 50 jobs created by an incubator client generate another 25 jobs in the community.

40 percent of incubators are technology focused; 30 percent are mixed use, accepting a wide variety of clients; and the remainder focus on service, light industrial and niche markets or on assisting targeted populations.

NBIA estimates that 75 percent of incubators are nonprofit and 25 percent are for-profit.

45 percent are urban, 36 percent are rural and 19 percent are suburban.

Your first step is to see if there is an incubator in your community. The yellow pages may have a listing or you can check with your local Chamber of Commerce or Small Business Administration. Get the name of the person who heads up the program and give him or her a call. Learn about the kinds of companies, organizations and opportunities which may exist.

Remember, entrepreneurs may be more likely to give you a shot if you have something to offer. Your contribution at this stage, coupled with dedication and loyalty, could play a vital role in the company's or organization's success. If you can contribute in this way, you have just created an exciting future for yourself.

Scan the Listings of New Vendors' Licenses in Your Local Newspaper

Another good source for finding entrepreneurs may be the listings of new vendors' licenses in your local paper. These names should represent a wide gambit of operations, from well-financed enterprises to sole proprietors operating off their kitchen tables. However, you never know what opportunities and relationships lie in seeking to help someone in his or her start-up venture.

Refer to SCORE, the Service Corps of Retired Executives

For more than twenty-five years, one of the most influential programs sponsored by the Small Business Administration has been SCORE—the Service Corps of Retired Executives. Through this program, people starting their own businesses receive free business counseling from fellow business professionals who are now retired. The new business person also can attend topical seminars for a modest fee.

SCORE is set up to provide free, experienced advice in practically every field there is, including high technology. SCORE counselors network with one another and often will team together to help each other's "clients."

If you are able to connect with a SCORE counselor, he or she may provide you the opportunity to be matched to an entrepreneur who can use your talents and skills. Contact your local Small Business Administration office and request more information about SCORE. A good place to start networking is to attend a SCORE seminar in your area which most closely matches your chosen career.

A Warning on Want Ads

Another place to look for job openings or internship positions is in newspaper classifieds or want ads. Sometimes, small businesses and start-up companies will advertise for help in this section. However, I would like to share with you an experience that I had with the want ads, so that you can learn to be savvy about how to read them.

During my first years of college, I worked at several kinds of jobs. I've told you about my experience as a pizza runner. I was also a grill cook, dish washer, photo-lab specialist (did I bomb on that one!) and a law clerk. While I did learn some important things on occasion, none of these jobs had much to do with my future career path.

Before I "networked" into my last position as a law clerk, I began searching the want ads, looking for something "better." I thought there had to be an opportunity out there that would help me advance to my ultimate career.

One day I opened the newspaper to the classifieds and saw a want ad that promised incredible results and rewards. You know the type. Unfortunately, I didn't. I rushed to the phone, called the number and was excited when they were willing to interview me the next morning.

Rising early, I got out my very best thrift store suit, got dressed, had a light breakfast and took off. I was not about to be late. I drove straight to their office in an industrial park. Walking in, I saw it was a small new office with hardly any furniture, and few people around who looked much older than age twenty-two.

The president's name was Norman. As he came towards me, I noticed he wore what I guess was supposed to be an impressive and expensive suit. Norman ushered me and another guy, Bob, into his office. I saw it was the only one with furniture. (Okay, they did have metal folding chairs and a card table in the waiting room.)

Norman's first question to me and the other person I was interviewing with was, "Do your cars run okay?" I nervously lied through my teeth.

Without telling us what the jobs entailed, Norman then bragged about his great "product," which he had stored in a warehouse across the street. We had no idea what this mysterious product was nor what it was for. We were both too stupid to ask.

Norman then began boasting that he owned not one, but *two* Mercedes Benz convertibles, both of which were parked right out front.

For the next few minutes, Norman talked and I pretended to listen. I was waiting to hear about the job. Then Norman finally said, "Alright. Now we are going to attend a marketing workshop!"

I thought we were going to another office. That was a mistake I would regret for the next eight grueling hours. After we left his office, Norman turned us over to another employee named "Steve-O."

My interviewing partner Bob and I got into a Pinto with Steve-O, who said he was taking us to a seminar on product marketing.

In reality, he kidnapped us to Lancaster, Ohio, a town thirty miles away. There, Steve-O went door-to-door peddling perfume clones—and telling blatant lies in his sales pitch—with us tailing behind him.

Over the next eight hours:
- We were thrown out of several business establishments, including the local mall.
- We were threatened with a gun.
- We were chased by a vicious guard dog.

All in very cold and rainy weather.

Bob and I became so frustrated and angry that we actually considered ditching Steve-O. Instead we suffered through the rest of the day with him.

When we finally got back to the office, I spoke not one word. I got into my car and drove straight home, feeling like a fool. A hard lesson was learned.

If you decide to use the want ads and find yourself seduced by ads that sound too good to be true, I have some news.

They almost always are too good to be true!

Let me give you some samples of the ads to avoid. These are actual classified ads taken from a recent Sunday newspaper. The names and phone numbers have been changed to protect the innocent. These ads are for bogus peddling positions, in the "General" category, with no base or benefits included. They are not legitimate sales positions, which would be listed under a category labeled "Sales & Marketing" or something similar:

FULL TIME - $580/WEEK
Due to recent expansion, local company has immediate
openings for 20 men and women. Start Tuesday morning.
No experience necessary, will train.

Must be neat in appearance and ambitious.
Management trainee positions open.
Call Monday only for interview. 555-8764

MANAGERS
Immediately hiring. No experience necessary.
Will train. Call Lisa. 555-4739.

How to Spot Bogus Peddling Want Ads

Bogus peddling ads have some distinct characteristics. Learn to spot them.

How Is the Ad Categorized?

They are usually listed, as I said before, in the "General" or "Miscellaneous" section of the help wanted ads. Most are not found where legitimate sales positions are posted.

How Much Money Do They Offer?

With no skills and no training, how can you expect to earn much more than five to eight dollars an hour? Bogus ads promise a pay scale usually twice as much as a real "no experience necessary" job would offer.

Interested in Management?

Often, these ads say they are looking for "managers," not sales people. Their rationale is you will be enticed by thinking you can become a manager instead of a salesperson with zero experience.

Don't Bother Writing Us—Call!

There is no address to send a resume. There is only a phone number, and an interview is very easy to schedule. You will most likely talk to someone who will schedule you for an appointment the very next day.

Titles Are Stressed over Work

There is no job description, only job titles. Remember, *titles are meaningless*. They hook kids who don't know any better by promising them glamorous titles, such as "manager" and "executive," but they won't say what's really involved (especially not over the phone).

So when scanning the want ads, beware. I hope that my ordeal will save you much time, frustration and gasoline in the future.

What Next? Here Are Some Steps You Can Take Today

1) As you network and talk to people, you may meet individuals from different types of business and organizational cultures. Take notice, and ask these people to describe for you the differences between their environments versus larger/smaller ones. Remember, the more you know about a particular company or organization's culture and atmosphere, the more accurately you can judge whether you'll fit in.

2) You will most likely have to do many different things in a single job, and you should want to. Moving sideways encompassing more territory, you can often make headway and clear a passage upward. It is important for you to begin diversifying your life experience as soon as possible. Always be on the lookout for opportunities to try new things.

3) Visit some local temp agencies and explore opportunities. Note what type of companies or industries they service.

4) Research small business incubators in your community and look into paying them visits.

5) Attend a business seminar sponsored by SCORE or your local Chamber of Commerce.

6) Attend a seminar on non-profit organizations. This could be a great way to meet with people involved in the local branches of these organizations.

7) Look into local chapters of professional associations and Rotary Clubs. They can be remarkable sources for networking and discovering opportunities within local businesses.

8

Short-term Work, Long-term Benefits: Internships and Summer Employment

"It's imperative to have internships and summer jobs, and to start on them as soon as possible."

> \- Kendra Frank
> *Capital University*
> *Broadcasting*

"In the competitive field of broadcasting and production, the prospect of landing a *full-time* job upon graduation is not really an issue," notes Kendra Frank, who works for a major network affiliate in Columbus, Ohio. "If you're lucky, you can get a part-time job, and if it works out well, six months to a year down the road you may land a full-time position. That's why it is imperative to have internships and summer jobs, and to start on them as soon as possible."

While in college, Kendra began using internships to explore what type of work she wanted to do. She obtained a particularly helpful internship with a local consulting firm doing video production. "That was a great experience," Kendra says enthusiastically. "I landed it with the help of my academic advisor, who knew the person who hired me. Through the intern program, I learned the basics of video production, from reviewing and logging footage to creating video edit lists for scripts and producing finished shows. It also gave me the first real exposure to seeing projects through from beginning to end. That's something which is often tough to get in the classroom."

Kendra worked on that internship up through and for several months following her graduation from college. Once she graduated, Kendra also took on a part-time summer job as a camera operator at the network affiliate, where she soon landed a full-time position.

"I worked in that summer position, along with my internship, for six to eight months. Today, I work at the station full time as morning news editor."

While the thought of working two part-time jobs may not sound enticing to some people, Kendra appreciates the way in which the two different environments complemented one another. "While everyone is professional in how they go about their work, the consulting firm was a much more formal environment than the television station. That was because there was a greater direct interaction with clients. So I was able to learn my craft from the perspective of two different environments."

"Also," she adds, "I can't stress enough the value of advisers and the career office. It was through my advisor that I got both the internship and the summer job. It seems that if the advisors get to know you better as a person, then they have a better idea of what opportunities might suit you. Also, they have more connections and can be a tremendous help to students looking for opportunities and for ways to meet people in the business community."

Overall, Kendra really believes in the value of internships and summer employment. As Kendra notes, "Having different experiences really allows you to be more sure about your decisions of what you want to do with your life."

Embracing a Pivotal Moment

As a student, whether you are of traditional age or are returning to school to begin a new career, you are at a pivotal moment in your life. Many business leaders have commented to me that how one spends (or should we say, "invests") his or her time as a student will have a tremendous impact on all the decades to follow.

This chapter focuses on *short-term* experiences which can have a *long-term* impact on your career and your life. I will show you how internships and summer employment can be great opportunities to gain experience, improve your education and build relationships, thus enabling you to jump-start your career.

Even though internships and summer jobs might only last a few months, in the minds of most people who will interview you, these positions equate directly with work experience. As you will soon find out when you enter the work world, experience is extremely important—all kinds of experience.

Up to this point, we have put a lot of emphasis on the value of volunteering. You have read about the many possibilities that exist for volunteers within small and large organizations and with start-up operations. By now you understand that you can start your career, even your first paying job, just by filling the needs of another person or organization. Most important, you know that through all these processes, *what is key is that you consistently act and work with integrity and you seek to benefit others and build relationships with those around you.*

Although volunteer work is often more long-term in nature, the same principles and values can be applied to short-term employment. As we saw with Kendra, after a few months of interning and working part-time, she was able to learn about her industry, pick up valuable job skills, meet people in her intended career field, and eventually, achieve full-time employment. As we examine internships and summer employment in more detail, you will see how you can benefit from these experiences, too.

Using Internships to Jump-Start Your Career

According to the National Society for Experiential Education, an internship is defined as a "carefully monitored work or service experience in which an individual has *intentional learning goals* and reflects actively on what he or she is learning through the experience."

Some of the key words listed here are *intentional learning goals*. Internships are viewed as an educational tool. Basically, your internship at a company or organization is a twofold transaction: you are there to get experience in a certain field or line of work, and the company or organization has an extra person around for a while to pitch in. The internship may or may not include a modest stipend. The internship might also earn you some college credits.

Structured internships are most often provided by mid-sized to larger companies. Many of these types of intern programs are offered by big-name companies which look good on resumes. So be prepared for competition which rivals that of full-time employment.

Should You Consider a Structured Internship Program?

This type of internship can be especially productive if:

1) *You are interested in developing specific skills.*

Internships are often *skill-specific*. For instance, as with Kendra, if you are majoring in broadcast video production and you want some experience in the various facets of production, then an internship may be a great place to start. It could be with a television station, a video production facility or an advertising/public relations agency.

Regardless of your major, an internship can provide your first chance to take the theory learned in the classroom and see how it applies—or does not apply—to the real world.

If you get into an internship program, make sure that specific goals are set and understood between you and your employer. You may go into it hoping to gain some specific experience or skill, but that may not be the goal in the mind of the employer. Understand that many larger firms are taking on interns to compensate for their reduced staffs. However, this doesn't mean that you are there solely to do mindless busywork. While some drudgery is to be expected, the bottom line is, *you are there to learn— not to be exploited*. So try to establish the goal up front.

2) *You are exploring a career in a specific field.*

Perhaps you want to know what it's like to work in a certain kind of profession or organization. An internship can give you a lot of on-the-job experience. In fact, it is becoming popular for many people—not just college students—who are thinking about changing careers to opt to do some internships in that particular field before making a final decision as to their futures.

3) *You want to build relationships with people within a particular professional community.*

Choosing an internship for this purpose can make a lot of sense. When I began to meet more people within the public relations/communications field, a startling revelation occurred to me: *these people all know each other!*

As you probably are aware by now, in some areas such as communications, film and media as well as certain professions and industries, these close relationships are very common. Structured internships can give you an introduction into these existing networks.

Further, these programs are an excellent way to meet a mentor who can continue to help and advise you after your internship ends. Many internships give students the opportunity for one-on-one guidance with a professional in the field. If you make use of your time to develop a connection with your mentor, this relationship can then form the basis for future support.

It is also important to stay in touch with all the people with whom you work. When your time of service is over, get names and addresses, and seek opportunities to keep the relationships alive.

4) *You realize compensation is not always financial.*

A key message of this chapter—and of this book—is about investing your time today for a payoff tomorrow. Waiting tables or flipping burgers may yield you a modest paycheck, and you can still develop interpersonal skills. But such occupations are not going to do much in the way of honing professional work skills or building relationships with people who can introduce you to new opportunities.

If you need an internship that offers a salary or a stipend, so be it. There are salaried internships available, which will probably pay on about the same scale as flipping burgers.

Just remember, the non-financial compensation internships offer in terms of building relationships, contacts and skills will be far greater than any dollar amount.

5) *You really want a big-name employer on your resume.*

Despite the fun often poked at it, name-dropping is and always will be a big game. Depending on your field, there may be some impressive companies, institutions or organizations which would bring star luster to your resume.

If this is the case, then think about which ones those would be. Are these companies located in the town in which you go to college or live? If not, do they sponsor interns from out-of-town? Many do.

In the resources appendix of this book, I've listed some internship guides and directories. Many of these will index companies, institutions and organizations by field. Use these resources to write to the companies and to learn what it takes to get into the programs to which you aspire.

6) *Your career or job goal requires a combination of experiences.*

In addition to whatever you are majoring in, whether it be science, medicine, education, law, accounting, communications, psychology, or anything else, there is one other field to which you should have exposure—business.

Contrary to what many people think, business is about much more than making money. First and foremost, business is about serving needs and making wise use of human and material resources. In legitimate business, profit is the by-product only when these two requirements are met. These principles apply not only to businesses and corporations. They also are appropriate for government agencies, churches, schools and non-profit organizations.

Whatever your course of study, learn the ABC's of business, and likewise, examine your career goals. Remember to keep this in mind when you are pursuing and researching internship opportunities.

Why Internships Are Growing

According to the National Society for Experiential Education, interning is up nearly 40 percent since the early 1990s. The greatest demand for internships appears to be in many of the emerging fields: the environment, health care, communications and international business.

More companies are offering internship programs, partly to make up for reduced labor but also because they find these programs help in identifying potential employees who are compatible to the people, culture and goals of their organizations. It is often less costly, more efficient and more insightful to "test" the abilities and attitudes of a temporary intern, rather than to interview a person two or three times and then hire that person on full time and hope for the best.

Another reason why internships are growing is that more people are taking them—and not just college students. As I previously mentioned, career changers and displaced professionals are a growing segment of those seeking experiences in different fields, in making new contacts, in gaining new skills and in being able to better evaluate their interests before—and not after—making a commitment.

The Real Question About Internships:
How to Get One

With the number of internships increasing all the time, there are more opportunities out there now than there ever were. Getting into one of these structured internship programs is not much different from applying for a job. For different programs at different companies, institutions and organizations, exact application procedures and requirements can vary. However, you can almost bet on needing the routine stuff: a resume and a cover letter.

Here are some steps you can take before applying:

1) *Decide what kind of skills or experience you need the most.*
The answer to this question either screams out at you or is quite fuzzy. If you are unsure of what field you should pursue, ask a teacher,

counselor, mentor or even a friend who shares a common frame of reference.

You can even do a survey of your skills. Determine how you would rank yourself in the following areas:

- Technical—be it general computer skills or those specific to your career
- Social/interpersonal—how much experience you have had working with other people
- Specific work skills—how much experience you have had with the career you are planning to do

2) *Check out some internship resources, on the web, at your library, or local career or academic department office.*

There are some very helpful guides on internship programs in this country and abroad, and they are all likely to be found at your campus or public library. The best ones are updated yearly, but if you can't find the most current, a one- or two-year-old edition should still do. I have listed a number of these resources in appendix 3, but I would like to mention some of my top choices:

National Directory of Internships compiled and published by the National Society for Experiential Education (www.nsee.org).

Peterson's Internships published annually with more than 40,000 opportunities listed (www.petersons.com).

The Internship Bible, by Mark Oldman and Samar Hamadeh. Published by the Princeton Review with more than 100,000 internships listed.

Internships by Sara Dulaney Gilbert. Published by Macmillan, with more than 25,000 opportunities described.

Many of these resources divide and cross-reference the listings by field or category, and many include additional helpful advice for applying. They also include an index of company and organization names. Most listings explain the role of the intern, the number of openings for applications, as well as any specific application requirements, such as chosen major or minimum GPA.

Do a quick Google (www.google.com) search under "internships" and countless sites will pop up, including the ones mentioned here and elsewhere in this book. Take a look at those resources available. Searching for the right opportunity can take a lot less time than it used to.

Your academic office and/or career office will likely also have a listing of available internships. Ask them about it.

3) *Seek out a handful of opportunities that you feel would be helpful, and go after them.*

Once you know what skills you want to develop, and you have gathered information about internships which could teach you these skills, then go after them! Follow application requirements to the letter. This is critical, especially in cases where competition is stiff. Employers receiving stacks of applications are looking first to weed out the definite rejects. Don't make their job any easier.

Before applying, try to gain an understanding of what the employer's needs are. Learn what you can about the employer. Identify your own past activities and experience which the organization may find appealing. Most important, though, is that you act with the same professionalism which would be expected of a job applicant, and that you project a positive, eager-to-learn attitude.

Also, visit your college department office and find out if the internship would qualify for course credit. If it does, there may be forms which your prospective employer will need to fill out.

You Can Design Your Own Internship!

Suppose you want to gain a certain type of experience, and you even know of a local company which you think could provide the perfect opportunity for you to do so. The problem is, that company does not offer any kind of internship program. What do you do next?

The answer is simple. You must design and propose your own internship program. Here are some steps you can take to accomplish this:

1) *Research similar internships—ones which suit you but are not available through companies in your community.*

Take a look at the listings in any of the previously suggested internship directories. Note how the intern programs are structured, whether they are paid or unpaid, and how long they last. Pay close attention to internship titles and specific job duties.

2) *Identify an employer or group of employers whom you feel may be a good match for doing this internship.*

The companies or organizations may be large, medium-sized or small. Once you have an employer in mind, you may first wish to try networking your way into the offices to talk with the people who make the decisions. Speak to your friends, teachers and family, and see if they know anyone working for the company. If this doesn't help, you can also use a variety of sources to research and put you in touch with a list of prospective employers, including:

- The nearest chapter of a professional organization
- Your local Chamber of Commerce
- Area small business incubators
- Local yellow pages or industrial directory (which can be found at your library)
- Various online business directories, found through library websites.

3) *Write a targeted proposal letter about what you would like to do.*

Once you know who to contact at the company, then write that person a letter—preferably not more than one or two pages.

Do not enclose a resume—that would be premature. Also, that person may glance at the resume and not the letter and then routinely file it (either in the cabinet or the trash) with no further thought.

Some key issues to address in your letter:

- *Briefly introduce yourself, your background and what you hope to learn from an internship.* You want to make a good first impression on your prospective employer. So, in a positive and direct manner, you want to tell a little about yourself and what you hope to achieve.

- *Try to give specific reasons why you are contacting this particular employer.* Acknowledge that you have been researching opportunities, yet did not find the employer listed as offering any intern programs. Nevertheless, explain that you have researched the company and feel that it could provide the right environment and opportunity for your professional growth.

- *Convey any relevant previous experience, especially anything which might serve the company's specific needs.* Ultimately, a busy person reading the letter is going to weigh the cost/benefit ratio of even considering your proposal. He will wonder, What's in it for me? *Why should I spend my time talking to this stranger?* Think of how you might answer these questions, and incorporate that information into the body of your letter. Be specific about what you want to do, which department you wish to work in, and how your internship will benefit both you and the company. This will indicate that you have done your homework and are serious about your intentions.

- *Think about offering your services for free.* Especially when working in a small business, a start-up or a non-profit organization, you can practically count on not receiving a wage. Fortunately, the experience you get may more than make up for any financial considerations. Larger firms may also wish to take you on for free. But you will encounter many large companies that have a standard policy *against* allowing people to work without pay. In this case, you may simply be punching a clock for five to seven dollars an hour.

- *Close your letter with a specific request.* You will want to meet with the person to whom you are writing to discuss this proposition further. A meeting is important. Even if the company does not take you as an intern, it is still an opportunity to make a contact. Perhaps the person you meet can point you in a helpful direction. In your letter, let the person know you will give him or her a call in a few days. And of course, provide the right information for your person to call you.

4) *Follow up.* If your letter said you would call at a certain time, then do it. If this whole concept sounds intimidating, you will be surprised at how receptive people usually will be to your proposal. Designing your own internship shows initiative and drive which may not be as visible were you applying from a mere directory listing or going through an established campus program. Initiative and drive are definitely qualities which a prospective employer wants in an employee!

More Short-Term Opportunities:
Summer Employment

First of all, there is no law which states you can't go to school in the summer. Most summers I took at least a few classes, just to keep up the pace. However, if you are planning to get away from the campus entirely, there is a whole world of opportunity that awaits you.

Many students take a variety of odd jobs during their college years. I know I did. I had friends who worked the same jobs full-time during the summers and part-time during the school year. That may have been a better strategy than what I chose, because after four years working at one place with the same group of people, my friends built some very solid relationships.

Your time in the summer or during any breaks is valuable and short-lived, and it is wise that you invest it more carefully, and with a greater goal in mind than just making a few bucks. Although money can be in many cases a serious consideration, it's not the prime one. Advancing your future career is.

Think of it as an Adventure

Have you ever thought about taking a job in which you:
- work as a park ranger preserving our nation's wilderness
- snap photos of amusement park visitors
- assist scientists as they collect nature samples
- work on board a cruise ship
- counsel and guide kids at a summer camp

This is just a sampling of the more exotic-sounding opportunities available to young people every summer. For organizations which operate camps, parks, and cruise ships, summer is the busiest season. These industries will need a lot of temporary workers to handle the extra business, and you can help fill these needs.

There is an endless array of positions available for summer employment, and not all of them are immediately obvious. For instance, the idea of leading thirty screaming kids in camp outings might not thrill you. But what if the camp had an opening in the head office? This would be a great opportunity to get some business management experience. Remember, the same organizations that need hands-on people to help with kids also have other needs which you can fill and problems that you can solve.

For another example, are you a computer guru? Do you like working with kids, but aren't very good at sports? Then how about teaching the kids computer skills for three months? You will be surprised at how much you learn, and also at how refined your own skills become by sharing them with others.

Where the Opportunities Are

When one thinks of summer employment, what often comes to mind are camps and amusement parks—organizations which cater to tourism and youth. From my own research, these organizations do seem to provide most of the summer opportunities *aimed specifically at young people.*

However, there are other organizations which offer summer employment, and thus very enriching and often different types of opportunities. Many of these positions provide on the job training, and require little or no previous experience.

Bear in mind: if you begin to research summer opportunities for yourself, you will likely find as many opportunities to wait tables and scrub toilets as you will the more exotic positions. What you decide to go with is up to you, but I would avoid work experiences that are no different from what you may get at a restaurant or shop up the street.

You want to come away from this experience with something more than pay stubs.

Among the organizations which employ summer workers are:

Summer Camps. There are summer camps in every state of the union. Many are geared to specific audiences, such as problem youths or kids with physical disabilities. Some are run by non-profits, such as YMCAs or the Boy Scouts. Others are run by churches and religious organizations. Still others are privately owned and operated.

Regardless of their affiliations or missions, collectively they offer perhaps the widest range of opportunities to students. If you want to take on a leadership role as a camp counselor, improve your abilities at a sport or a craft, or better develop your skills in human interaction and relationships, *all of these opportunities, and more* exist at summer camps.

Conference Centers. These are often located in remote areas, and many are open and running all year round. The types of people you would work with here are mainly from business and community groups. Conference centers provide these groups with places to hold meetings, conferences, parties and other events. If you are interested in event management as a possible career, a conference center might be the perfect place for you to learn more about this.

Environmental Programs and Organizations. Owned and operated by either government, educational or non-profit organizations, these provide many jobs for students interested in science, nature and preservation of the environment and wildlife. Opportunities may include on-site research and public education activities as well as general business and office functions.

State and National Parks offer opportunities similar to those available through environmental programs and organizations.

Tourist Attractions and Expeditions. These are organizations which arrange tours in different parts of the country for foreign visitors.

Tour guides are in big demand during the summer and over holidays. If you are bilingual, or have strong background knowledge of your region or country, then this could be a great job for you. It could also help you better develop your skills in communication and in leadership.

Ranches. While many seek people to do cooking and cleaning work, tourist ranches are also on the lookout for experienced wranglers. If this was something you wanted to eventually learn—without majoring in equestrian studies—then looking after the horses may be a first step toward getting to ride them. Be on the lookout for administrative and events opportunities at ranches, as well.

Theme Parks. A roommate of mine in college who enjoyed photography spent three summers in a row working at Kings Island, photographing visitors as they entered the park. That's all he did, and he loved it.

While theme parks have plenty of food-service, janitorial and housekeeping positions to fill, they also offer opportunities in administration, marketing, and coordinating events. Some parks may have educational and arts positions open, depending upon their actual "themes."

Volunteer Opportunities. Student-based organizations such as Campus Outreach Opportunity League are offering more and more summer and spring break volunteer activities. As service learning continues to grow along with campus-based service learning organizations, be on the lookout for new and exciting volunteer opportunities popping up. These include working in rural areas to rebuild homes for poor people, or serving inner-city youths in educational or community-based restoration projects.

A Few Tips on Landing That Right Summer Job

Overall, the process of landing summer positions in areas that may yield future employment benefits is really no different from applying for a longer, more permanent job. Here are some points to follow if this is something you are considering:

1) *Hit the books.*

Review a summer job directory, such as Peterson's *Summer Jobs for Students,* or one of the others I have listed in appendix 3. Get want ads from newspapers in areas you live in or want to live in this summer. Also, scrutinize your campus newspaper and bulletin boards around the college. Late winter/early spring is when the requests for summer help start to come in.

2) *If you want to be working by June, don't wait until May to send in your application!*

By that time, the most interesting and beneficial positions are usually filled. It is probably advisable to start sending in your resumes and application letters by the end of March.

Of course, this can be tricky. We could say, "the sooner the better." However, if you send in your packet too soon and the organization is not yet preparing its summer employment roster, then your application can get thrown to the bottom of the pile!

My advice: when you find some organizations or positions to which you would like to apply, but it is still pretty early in the year, call the company and find out when would be the best time to send in your application. You can also use this call as an opportunity to confirm your contact's name and address, and to find out a little more about the position for which you are applying.

3) *Don't worry if you cannot list any relevant experience on your resume.*

For your purpose, a resume should be one page, detailing any relevant background and/or experience. If you don't have a lot of experience, don't worry. Most summer employers don't expect it unless they specifically state otherwise.

Be sure to include all outside activities—volunteer and educational—in addition to any past employment. List your primary areas of study in school, and note any classes which may be relevant to the position for which you are applying. Identify any computer or other technical skills you may have. For instance, can you fix your own car? If so, let them know!

While it is not customary, listing three or four references is recommended by many counselors. These references can be people who may have employed you or counseled you—anyone who is older with whom you have established a relationship.

It is helpful for employers to know that others will readily vouch for your good character. And including references will make your application stand out from the rest—especially if the employer is receiving applications from students all over the country. Just be sure that the people you list as references have given you their permission to be contacted.

What If an Internship or Summer Job Is Not Meeting Your Expectations?

In most situations, what you gain from an experience is really up to you. You decide how an experience will affect you. Yes, you may feel in some internships or summer positions that an employer is not meeting his obligations to you, but you will *always learn something*—it just may not be what you had in mind.

For instance, a friend of mine named Craig once took an internship to get some experience with certain computer skills. That was the goal in his mind, and it may very well have been the intention of the executive who hired him to help Craig achieve this goal. However, Craig's wishes were not a concern of the territorial and controlling supervisor under whom my friend was placed.

Although Craig was disappointed that he was not allowed much time at the computer, he eventually realized that he did learn something important at his internship. Instead of gaining experience in computer programming, Craig instead gained valuable insights on dealing with difficult people in the office.

If you do not feel in your heart that your internship or your summer job is giving you as much as you had hoped, you have some options:

- If it is a short-term assignment (say three months), do your best and stick it through. At least you have gained resume experience. Meanwhile, start looking for your next opportunity.

- If it is a longer assignment and you are not being paid, then walk. But be sure to give plenty of notice and be respectful of the employer's needs. If you have the opportunity, clearly let him or her know why the experience is not meeting your expectations.
- Talk to your boss and try to work things out. The problem may be one of miscommunication, and your employer may not realize that you are unhappy. See if you can schedule a meeting with your supervisor to find a solution to the problem. It never hurts to try, and what have you got to lose?

What Next? Here Are Some Steps You Can Take Today

1) Much of this chapter emphasizes the value of working in more meaningful employment than the typical summer job. But let's face it: some of you are doing just that. You know that you need to get into something more beneficial, but either you are too comfortable staying where you are, you procrastinate, or perhaps you just can't work these steps into your busy schedule.

   If this is the case, here's my advice: quit your menial job.

   Now you have some time! Now procrastination is not so easy! Once you quit that dead-end job, re-read this chapter and the rest of this book, and get your career rolling.

2) While I try not to emphasize resumes too much in this book, you will need to have one, whether you apply for an internship or summer job. If you haven't drafted one yet, give it a shot. Treat it like a brainstorming session. You may be surprised at all that you have accomplished in your life.

   As to the dos and don'ts of resume-writing, as far as I am concerned, there is no clear-cut way to do it. If you want a book that shows you how, you will find *hundreds* of these at the library. Pick one that has been published recently.

3) Take an inventory of your abilities. What skill do you lack that could have a strong impact on your success in your future career? Focus on opportunities that allow you to develop that skill.

4) Talk to fellow students who have done internships or summer jobs in your field. How was the experience for them? What would they recommend? What would they avoid? *Who do they know?*

5) Review the directories mentioned in this chapter and in appendix 3. Get a directory from your local Chamber of Commerce. After reading these, have you found any companies at which you would like to intern or work for the summer? See if the companies list their programs at your college career office.

Read what's available, and make a resolution to continue reading. You'll be astounded at all the opportunities waiting for you.

9

Service Learning: Education Through Experience

"Service learning allows you to really see the difference you can make, and to reflect on those experiences with others."

\- Jeremie Maehr
Case Western Reserve University
Civil (Environmental) Engineering

From the time he was a child, Jeremie Maehr had a keen interest in the environment. "When I was very young growing up in New Jersey," Jeremie recalls, "the water in our neighborhood was contaminated by harmful, toxic waste dumping."

Experiences tied to this event enlightened Jeremie as to how information—its presence or lack thereof—influenced how people reacted to various crises. As a result, during his freshman year at Case Western Reserve University, Jeremie became involved with the university's Center for the Environment, building community awareness of environmental issues in Cleveland neighborhoods. Jeremie also joined the CWRU's Office of Student Community Service and AmeriCorps to continue addressing local environmental needs. Jeremie organized fellow student volunteers to collect and analyze soil samples, and to conduct education programs for inner-city children.

"One week, I attended a series of lectures where students could interact and discuss environmental issues with scientists, engineers, and community leaders," Jeremie says. "It was through this that I became acquainted with the Center for the Environment's director, and was then offered an internship in the office of Environmental Service Learning."

Of Service Learning, Jeremie says, "It provides a perspective on your work which you don't get from the classroom, alone. I remember during my senior year, I was working with a team of other students on a community-based, watershed, service learning program. As we were taking measurements and making calculations, which would then be passed on for use by engineers, I will never forget what a fellow student told me. She said, 'Even though I have done all the chemical analysis, I'm still worried about the accuracy of the results.'"

"The point was, our work wasn't a lab experiment, it was real. Lives were going to be affected by what we did, and how well we did it."

Jeremie's advice to other students: "Service Learning allows you to really see the differences you can make, and to reflect on those experiences with others. You make friends and build relationships with people, many of whom will really work to help you when you need it. But to build trust, you must always be honest. Ask questions. If you don't have answers, admit it. And be open to other people's opinions, even if they contradict your own."

Jeremie's many environmental service activities have earned him multiple recognitions, including the Ambassador Award by Ohio Campus Compact in 1997. Today, he continues his work in both service learning and environmental education as Assistant Director of Environmental Service Learning at Case Western Reserve University. "I guess I can be an example of how service learning can lead *directly* to career opportunities," Jeremie says, "since I was working at this job as an intern before I even graduated."

Jeremie brought up several good points about the value of combining service with education. Many colleges and universities across the nation are beginning to recognize these points, which is why they are now incorporating **Service Learning** into their academic curriculums.

Service Learning is a growing philosophy and practice which recognizes the important role that public and community service can play in education. In simple terms, Service Learning, through first-hand experience, shows students how their talents and efforts can be applied to improve other people's lives and better their communities. This experience also helps students develop values that stress social responsibility.

Service Learning can be implemented in a variety of ways. Sometimes it is through a supplementary activity within a classroom-based course. Sometimes it is a course itself. Often a student will earn some academic credit for a specified number of hours served every week.

How Does Service Learning Differ from Ordinary Internships or Voluntary Action?

In the many academic volumes and articles that have been written on Service Learning over the years, you may see dozens of different answers to this question. But actually, Service Learning does not "differ" from regular internships or volunteerism. It is more of an *extension* of both, taking the best points of each, combining them and filling in the gaps. Thus, through Service Learning, you can have the best of both worlds.

Like an internship, Service Learning allows a student to perform work that relates specifically to his or her intended vocation, thereby enhancing that student's professional skills. Service Learning programs, like some internships, often give course credit, and they usually provide students with the advice of a professional in the field.

Like a volunteer program, the Service Learning experience turns the whole world into a classroom. Service learners often *see* the value and difference their efforts play in other people's lives and in the community. As with volunteering, students in Service Learning programs will also develop skills that employers seek out universally.

PRAXIS: From Theory to Practice, Back to Theory

Praxis is an academic term which describes the relationship between action and theory in the learning experience. Because it is important not just to take action, but to contemplate that action and the results, many Service Learning programs include a periodic time of reflection in which you can both share your experiences with fellow teachers and students, and hear about their experiences in return.

Thus, a student, upon learning a theory, has the chance to apply that knowledge through action. Afterward, the student returns back to the classroom where he or she may reflect on and dissect that experience, and then use it to develop even more refined theories. Those theories are then shared with the rest of the class.

For the students who participate in praxis, their time of reflection will not necessarily require them to revise theory taught only in the classroom. Rather, by reviewing and sharing their service experiences for themselves and for their colleagues, the students gain a deeper insight into how their service affects them as well as the community.

Custom-Designed to Suit All Those Involved

Most of all, Service Learning programs are specifically designed to benefit the student *and* the community. Instructors will often go out to the community and determine what needs exist that their students can fulfill in a mutually beneficial way, and then develop a specific program from there.

Among the universities and colleges now using the Service Learning approach to solve a variety of community problems are:

- **Providence College**. Here, students studying American Public Policy learn firsthand the *consequences* of public policy, both good and bad (although that is something they must often decide for themselves). Students can serve meals at a homeless shelter, tutor in an urban school, interview welfare recipients and prepare case profiles for welfare reform.

- **Rhode Island School of Design**. Students conduct weekly art classes at the bedsides of hospitalized children, and also for senior citizens.
- **Wilmington College**. Business students are able to help develop business and marketing plans for local businesses and non-profit organizations.
- **Shawnee State University**. Science students participate in ecological projects to learn the applications for the study of science and nature.
- **Calvin College**. Those studying mathematics and computer science analyze demographic data from several food pantries to find patterns in the pantries' patrons. Seasonal and other variations were also considered to help predict when periods of high demand would arise.

Does Your School Have a Service Learning Program?

As of now, fewer than a thousand colleges and universities across the country have officially adopted Service Learning programs but the number is growing. Organizations such as **Campus Compact** (www.compact.org) and the **National Society for Experiential Education** (www.nsee.org) exist to support educators in their efforts to develop Service Learning programs.

However, each institution's program is usually much different from those found at other schools. For instance, college credit is usually granted to students participating in Service Learning projects. But not all schools offer credit.

There are many reasons why Service Learning programs differ from school to school and even department to department. Often, the differences occur *because the program itself is in its infancy*. Service Learning is still a relatively new philosophy in higher education. Different schools have different levels of funding available, as well as various numbers of people behind it. Most often, a college will become involved in Service Learning when an individual or small group of faculty members decides to try it out.

After receiving approval and funding for Service Learning programs, schools typically start them only for the disciplines where community service opportunities are most apparent, such as for education and psychology. Then, as the participation and interest grows throughout the college and the community, dialogue between community-based organizations and college staff may increase. Additional Service Learning opportunities then develop from there for other career disciplines, such as engineering, business and the arts.

You Can Develop Your OWN Service Learning Program

As I mentioned before, many of those in higher education still regard Service Learning as being in its infancy. But these educators are also beginning to recognize the value of turning the world into their students' classroom.

If you are interested in taking part in Service Learning, but your school hasn't set up a Service Learning program yet, don't despair. Maybe **you** can pioneer the program at your college or university. Since a lot of educators and administrators are becoming more interested in Service Learning, it should not be hard to find people at your school who would support your endeavor and help you design a program.

How do you start? The secret is in recognizing **opportunity** and acting upon it. For instance:

- An **accounting** student may see an opportunity to investigate loan and credit discrimination on behalf of the poor or to help a local organization obtain financing for community improvement projects.
- An **agriculture** student can help establish a community gardening project or aid in dietary planning for local agencies.
- A person studying to be an **architect** can help coordinate a local fix-up project. I was once involved in a project where a young, student architect directed us in repairing the roof for a church that was the home of an extensive Head Start program. Without the new roof, the kids would have had nowhere to go.

- Students majoring in **marketing or business** can do much to increase the bottom line of local groups, organizations and small businesses.
- **Chemistry** students can learn some of the effects that substance abuse has on individuals by serving in counseling and drug-treatment centers.
- Those students majoring in **computer information technology** have the chance to teach computer basics at just about any community center in any town in the country. People are desperate to learn these skills, which are crucial to job marketability. These students can also show people the right and wrong way to use computer technology.
- People majoring in **economics** have a tremendous doorway to opportunity in front of them. They can professionally serve consumer groups, small business organizations and local Goodwill agencies. Their knowledge of economics can help troubled people see new solutions to their money problems.
- The **Education** major can open up another gold mine of opportunities. Head Start programs, for example, will welcome those with teaching skills with open arms. Tutoring for older adults or prison inmates is another project an education student can take on.
- Students studying **engineering** may find some interesting needs for their design talents in helping those who are disabled or their scientific and environmental skills in working to improve the environment.
- Just as much as they need business majors, organizations of every kind require the skills of those studying **journalism and English**. The newsletter I edit utilizes writers from all over our town, and all are volunteers. Every group and organization must communicate to their clients and constituents. Your help in producing marketing communications can be an invaluable service.
- **Fine arts** students may wish to consider art therapy for those with mental disabilities. For example, my wife—an Illustration major—assisted at art therapy sessions with criminal offenders while she was in college.

- Those majoring in **health and recreation**, may find needs for their talents at a local hospital or community recreation center. You can also assist with or coordinate projects that teach healthy lifestyles, wholesome eating habits and safe recreation.
- **History** students may find use for their abilities at a local historical society, museum or library.
- I have a friend who recently finished his **law** degree, and while in school he would give general legal advice to people at a local homeless shelter. Educating the public on basic legal issues and concepts is a tremendous way to serve, as well as learn.
- **Psychology** students can also begin working professionally in many ways. Activities include research, counseling and organizational work.

What Service Learning comes down to is students and teachers recognizing a community need and responding to it. Perhaps you might see such a need that you, or even your whole class, can take on. Mention those opportunities to your teachers.

Take the initiative, provide leadership and make it happen.

What Next? Some Steps You Can Take Today

1) Talk to your advisor, your professors or other people on staff at your school. Find out what kind of Service Learning opportunities are available. Ask about getting involved.

2) If you have friends who go to other colleges or universities, find out what kinds of Service Learning programs are offered at your friends' schools. This could give you some good ideas about how to start and design a similar program for your own school.

3) Look around your community. Are there any obvious problems which need solving? Can you think of a way to help? If so, in addition to talking about your proposal with your advisor or

professor, you might also present your Service Learning ideas to community leaders like the local mayor or city council people. These leaders could marshal a lot of community support for your program. This is also a great way to meet people and network!

Hire Yourself!
Start Your Own Business

"We had to fold, but so what? I still regard it as a great accomplishment, and I'm proud of it. No one can take that away from me."
- Mark P. Kelnhoffer
Ohio Dominican College
Accounting and Business

Mark P. Kelnhoffer turned what began as a small college project into a professional organization of nearly 800 entrepreneurs from all over Ohio, six other states and sixteen universities.

"In the beginning, my friends and I were holding weekly meetings, each with a professional speaker addressing specific topics such as planning, marketing and cash flow management," Mark recalls. "Our initial plans were to establish a small, campus-based club of college students who were interested in learning about starting their own businesses.

"To get the word out, we sent media packets to regional newspapers and broadcast stations. Before we knew it, interest flourished beyond the campus, and we were up and running with monthly meetings in ten cities across Ohio. I had no idea it would grow so much."

For four years, the Ohio Entrepreneurship Association hosted a multitude of speakers, offered member discounts for services such as car rentals and provided resources and information through its vast network of business professionals and its monthly newsletter.

"We had many meetings of small business owners sharing stories of successes and pitfalls," Mark continues. "It was somewhat different from your average class or seminar. Members were able to hear about real situations and companies. It was a great learning opportunity for those interested in starting their own businesses."

Mark, who works today as a financial analyst, feels that one of the best things you can do as a student in order to learn and jump-start your career, is to start your own business or challenge yourself in some way that reaches beyond the classroom. "If nothing else, it can be a great experience to learn what it's like to have to wear many hats and put yourself in an employer's perspective."

Other tips Mark adds are the importance of believing in yourself and in what you can offer. "Do the best work you can," he says. "Deliver on what you promise and operate with integrity."

And what of the Ohio Entrepreneurship Association today? "After four years of tireless devotion, in March of 1995 I had to fold the operation due to funding difficulties. We weren't a 'business' in the normal sense. Rather, we were a 501(c)3 non-profit organization. Our services and programs, which on top of monthly meetings included a newsletter and online bulletin board, ate most of our operating expenses, which came from a $75 annual membership fee. Neither I nor my support staff—and we were all volunteers—could afford to keep working it."

Does Mark have any regrets? "It was a great experience," he says. "We helped a lot of people, met many others and really made an impact. We had to fold, but so what? I still regard it as a great accomplishment, and I'm proud of it. No one can take that away from me."

Mark's experience was one of tremendous growth and challenge. By creating an organization in which he built relationships with small-business people from all over the state, he learned much more than if he had chosen to merely go to school. Mark is a man who always sees options. As long as there is a need to be filled, he will be successful. This is the essence of entrepreneurialism.

If you are having trouble finding the right person to hire you, maybe you should stop searching for an outside source and start looking in the mirror.

Get to Know the Person Who Will ALWAYS Hire You

The student prepared for self-employment is best prepared to seek employment from others. Challenging students to think of economic independence calls forth resourcefulness, imagination, initiative and determination, qualities that are so often missing when they are simply looking for jobs. It encourages and hones the ability to promote oneself and builds confidence. In this way the person learns to search out someone to employ him or her and begins to tap his or her own potential for accepting broad responsibilities and creating rewarding self-made challenges. [1]

I only wish I could say this as succinctly as Jerry W. Gustafson does. His article, published in the *Journal of Career Planning and Employment*, goes on: "The better prepared you are to be self-employed, the better prepared you will be to seek employment from others, and the better off you will be if you are cut loose."

That's why you must become very familiar with the person who will ALWAYS give you a job: YOU!

One of the best things about entrepreneurship is the fact that it can offer so many rewards, yet is not restrictive to anyone. You can even start while you are still in school. In fact—let me repeat this— *don't wait until you graduate!*

Some of you may look at the heads of companies and see established professionals who appear really successful. You might feel somewhat envious of their wealth and renown. You may hope to be just like them one day—earning lots of money, driving a fancy car and living in a nice home.

Believe it or not, many of them might look at you with similar feelings. Seeing you and your peers, they may say to themselves, "Wow, those kids have their whole lives ahead of them. They probably do not have any responsibilities except keeping roofs over their heads. They can do whatever they want, whenever they want."

The truth is, many people who appear successful do not feel that way. They may have high-paying jobs, but those jobs may consume their life energy so that they no longer enjoy their careers. Some may feel trapped because of financial and personal obligations that hinder them from considering doing anything else with their lives. *They are afraid to take risks.*

Some people may disagree with me, but I think taking risks when you are young is easier than taking risks when you are old. The older you are, often the more you have, and thus *the more you have to lose.*

Entrepreneurialism Is Exploding

Big business is getting smaller, and small businesses are becoming more numerous. If you are someone who is beginning your career, and you want to try developing a business rather than working for someone else, it may help you to know that self-employment is growing. Why this growth in entrepreneurialism? There are a multitude of reasons:

Displacement

Downsizing, technological advancements and a growing supply of workers in some industries have all lead to a shrinking of opportunities in the traditional job market. Recessions, like the one during the early 1990s, also lead to a loss of employment as businesses folded or fired many of their employees to cut costs. It should be noted that during the 1990s recession, people were going solo and starting their own businesses in record numbers.

Disenchantment

To many people, going the traditional job-hunting search—finetuning the resume, looking snappy and having all the right answers for that job interview—has even less appeal now than ever. Therefore, some people are asking themselves: Must we have jobs to earn livings? The reply many of them are coming up with is "No."

As I mentioned earlier, a few years ago I was without a steady, full-time job for over six months. Although I had two job offers to choose from when I went back to full-time work, there were times when I really didn't think anything was going to come through. However, I took steps and was prepared to go out on my own if necessary.

Although my personal and family circumstances really required a more steady paycheck, I had reasons for giving serious consideration to starting my own business. While I waited for offers from other companies, I kept asking myself, *How much longer is this agony going to last before someone decides to hire me?*

By regarding traditional employment as my only option, I was surrendering control of my own and my family's future to someone else.

More and more people have had enough of the traditional employment route. A lot of people feel the same way that I did. This is one of the reasons why close to half a million small businesses are launched every year, and it is predicted that that number may double in the next few years.

Higher Education

Even institutes of higher education, as you may guess from reading about Jerry Gustafson's idea at the beginning of this section, are increasingly promoting entrepreneurialism in both the profit and non-profit zones as a viable career option. This is especially true of the business schools. More than a third of the country's top business schools have developed programs in entrepreneurship.[2]

Professional Freedom

For some people, self-employment may be a less-desired alternative to a steady job. For others, it can be the achievement of personal and professional freedom.[3]

At times, structured career planning can be futile because it depends so much upon the decisions and aspirations of others. It takes random meetings and being in the right place at the right time. Within a structure of a large company, politics can block an employee's way.

An individual can do the work, but someone else may take the credit. As an employee, you may provide a definite benefit and have it go unnoticed.

There are others who are tired of the "9 to 5" mentality. They don't want to be boxed in by a lot of corporate rules and regulations and office politics. These people include baby boomers as well as today's young, emerging professionals. They want to lead more fulfilling lives. They are being called "quality of life" people.

Adopting an "entrepreneurial mind-set" to developing a career means taking charge, assuming responsibility and making things happen. Entrepreneurs don't and can't blame others for their problems. They find detours around the political roadblocks and look for opportunities. They take calculated risks when necessary.[4]

For these people, the challenges are the price they pay for freedom. And it can definitely be worth it.

Regardless of the reasons for the boom of entrepreneurship, the Small Business Administration has recognized this growth. The administration is now providing even greater benefits and services to entrepreneurs, because in many ways *our country's economic future is in their hands*. These new entrepreneurs will make the breakthroughs, will provide services, and in many cases, will provide the new jobs.

Remember, this country was built by people who saw problems as opportunities. That tradition is still strong today.

Why You MUST Become an Entrepreneurial Student

Patience is a virtue, but too much of it leads to complacency and stagnation.

When I was growing up, I was taught to be patient. I even remember my mother nudging me in the movie theater while we were watching *The Empire Strikes Back*. The old and wise Jedi Master Yoda was telling Luke Skywalker to have patience. Yoda stressed its importance to achieve one's goals. Mom nudged me to make sure I was listening to Yoda.

Yes, patience is a virtue. To be patient is to plan and anticipate the long-term benefits of the sacrifices—the investments—we make today. To be patient is to be able to forego immediate gratification, to pass up making a quarter today so we can earn a dollar tomorrow.

However, some people are too patient. They sit around waiting for phones to ring, for their proverbial ships to come in. What they don't realize is that their ships will most likely never leave port if they don't take charge of the helm and plot a course to reach the desired destination.

To be entrepreneurial is to be proactive, not reactive. It is to constantly be seeking new opportunities to benefit someone else as well as yourself, and to be recognized for your special abilities.

To be entrepreneurial takes four traits: creativity, responsibility, flexibility and goal setting. Let's look at them one by one.

Creativity

You must not become so used to "following the program." Dr. E. Gordon Gee, a former president of Ohio State University, made an interesting comment in a radio interview regarding the emphasis on "proficiency" in the educational environment.

Proficiency, he asserted, measures one's ability to memorize and follow simple directions. But great proficiency does not always equate with actual *thinking skills*.[5]

To think, Gee countered, is to be creative. To think is to analyze a problem and figure out your own solution, and not just rely on someone else's answer. While it is important to consider outside sources of information, they must only contribute to your decisions, not make them for you.

This chapter focuses on the fact that we are all faced with the responsibility to support ourselves and earn our livings in this society. Too often, it has been "dictated" to many of us that there is one single, safest, most secure way to accomplish this: *by getting a job from an existing company.*

Now I am not knocking this type of traditional employment. It is important to our economy. I think that many people would prefer a stable job at a stable corporation to provide for themselves and for their families.

But this should never be regarded as the only solution, especially in these times. The fact is, if you don't have a traditional job to earn a paycheck, *there are still opportunities to earn profits.*

To figure out how, you must realize that it takes creative thinking to recognize entrepreneurial opportunities.

Once you find them, you are on your way to starting your own business.

Responsibility

When you start thinking for yourself and making decisions independently, you are taking responsibility for your own life. You are assuming the risk and accepting the reward.

We talked before about the importance of personal responsibility—and not blaming someone else for your mistakes or problems. An entrepreneur knows that things rarely turn out the way they are planned. The sooner you realize this and learn to anticipate problems, the easier your life and work will be for you when things go awry. And believe me, they will.

Acknowledging your own responsibility for what you do and who you are can be very liberating. In today's world, it's easy to feel like "the victim." Believe me, I know. That's just how I felt when I was standing in the unemployment line and struggling to find work.

It might be quite natural to feel victimized when something out of your control ruins your plans. But feeling that way doesn't help you to pick up the pieces and move on. Remember, you have the power to make the most of your opportunities. So in business, as well as in life in general, realize that you are making your own decisions and accept responsibility for the results of those decisions.

Flexibility

You have to realize that there may be more than one pathway to a predetermined goal. You are on a road, and that road may have detours, twists and turns. Expect the unexpected and be ready to make the most of it. Learn to adapt to change.

Remember that being flexible includes considering other options besides that of traditional employment in order to earn your living and build your career. Don't ever limit your options. Doing so will only limit your growth, career and achievements.

Goal Setting

The road you take must have a destination. Setting goals is extremely important, though you must make allowances for detours. I know that setting them can be most difficult, especially when you are just starting out.

Consider a Yale University study of its 1953 graduates: All of them were asked if they had a clear, specific set of goals written down with a plan to achieve them. Only 3 percent had. Twenty years later, the researchers followed up on those same graduates and discovered that the 3 percent with written goals were worth more financially than the entire other 97 percent combined![6]

Why is this? A friend reviewing an early draft of this book posed an interesting question: Does this mean that goals are the *cause* or the *effect* of personal drive and motivation? You might ask, *Which comes first?*

For most people, I think the goal comes first. It's a spark which ignites a fire in one's heart. It gives a person something to focus on, to refine and to nurture. By investing time and energy into a goal and into a plan to reach it, you give yourself the motivation and the direction to pursue that end.

Think about what you want to accomplish and plan how you might get there. And remember the other keys to success: flexibility, responsibility and creativity.

First Questions for the Budding Entrepreneur

According to Steve Mariotti, founder and president of the National Foundation for Teaching Entrepreneurship and author of *The Young Entrepreneur's Guide to Starting and Running a Business*, if you are considering the prospect of starting your own business while in college, there are two questions you should ask yourself. Both make up the process he refers to as "Opportunity Recognition."

The first question is internal. You must ask yourself, "What do I care about?" You must look within yourself, your hobbies, interests and values to determine what type of work or activity you enjoy or find rewarding.

Then, once you have looked within yourself, you must look to the marketplace. In your community, you must ask yourself what needs people have for which you can provide. Remember, we have already established that we live in a world full of needs.

The process of Opportunity Recognition is that of balancing the needs of others with your own personal ones, so that you are fulfilling both at the same time. This is very important. This is what makes your work more rewarding and helps you become more successful.

It's More Than Just the Money

Many of today's successful entrepreneurs will tell you that, while they may have achieved financial independence, the desire for money alone is not enough of a reason to start your own business. Why is that?

When I was in art school studying to be a graphic designer, I knew the field was very competitive. Some of my closest friends were among the best and most talented people around. I knew that I had talent. However, there was one other trait I noticed among the others which I did not have: *passion*. Passion for art, that is.

To be truly successful at anything, whether it is in business, parenting, a hobby, or any other role in life, you must have a fire in your belly. You must be able to commit to something for the long-term and make that commitment from the bottom of your heart.

It's passion which gets you up in the morning, ready to be and do your best.

It's passion which enables you to see beyond the roadblocks standing in front of you.

It's passion which tells you that what you are doing is worthy of your commitment, even though other people in your life may be telling you that you are wasting your time.

So ask yourself: *What do I care about? What gets me excited?* If you're not committed to something, you probably are not going to be successful—or happy.

This doesn't mean that a business or profession has to be exciting or glamorous; you can run a successful business hauling garbage. Many of today's wealthiest people weren't involved in Hollywood-like enterprises.[7] They held occupations such as construction contractors, restaurant operators, pest controllers, junk haulers and consultants.

The trait most common to all of them was that *they were entrepreneurs.* They sold products or services that *added value* to the lives of others. That alone is something to be excited about, and it was this sense of the value of their enterprises that enriched their hard work and long hours.

This issue is very important and should not be underestimated. Without these traits, your zest for what you're doing will lose its luster awfully fast. An enterprise should offer you more rewards besides money. There needs to be personal satisfaction, a sense of worth and contribution to the lives of others.

Ideas for Your Business

If you're still in college, remember that you are not necessarily embarking upon the enterprise which will last for the rest of your life. Maybe that's not what you want right now. But remember, once you open your own business, *you are planting and cultivating the seeds of your career.*

Are you having trouble figuring out what to do? Allow me to pose a question. As you were growing up, did you ever:

- Baby-sit?
- Mow lawns?
- Deliver newspapers?

If you did, you had your own business. From seventh through eleventh grade, I delivered newspapers every afternoon after school and on Sunday mornings. I also remember that my best friend and his brother had a pretty lucrative lawn-mowing business. They even went out and purchased their own lawn mowers and drove them to jobs in a car which they shared. They did this for several years and were very successful.

Are they still mowing lawns today? No, they've pursued other careers. But that early experience taught them a lot about responsibility and business—not to mention that it helped them pay the tuition for school.

Of course, that's not to say that mowing lawns and yard care isn't lucrative and can't be expanded into a career. A member of my church owns his own lawn maintenance business and has several employees. He is very successful.

What I recommend is that you start with something you enjoy and are good at, and go from there. For instance, do you excel at a particular school subject? If so, build on that excellence and start a tutoring service.

There are plenty of good books, guides and resources to help you develop ideas for starting your own business. These include books on planning, financing and marketing which can be found in your local library or bookstore. I've discussed several of these resources in greater detail in appendix III.

Entrepreneurship: Pros and Cons

There are traits and principles behind entrepreneurialism which I believe you must adopt, regardless of what you intend to do in life. Whether you are going to work in a traditional job or own your own business, you must still adopt an entrepreneurial spirit. This entails assuming responsibility for your life no matter what happens to you, as well as constantly looking for opportunities to serve others' needs.

However, when contemplating whether owning your own business as a career track, there are many points you must consider. Running your own business has its advantages and disadvantages.

Disadvantages

Insecurity. The fact is this: some small businesses fail. When this happens, your income disappears. That can be frightening.

In my work with non-profit organizations, I deal with freelancers quite often. I remember one telling me that his business is like a roller coaster. It is normally feast or famine. There are months when business, and thus his income, is down. Other months he gets so busy he can barely keep up.

These issues are most critical during the start-up phase of running a business. It's often in the first couple of years when you are building customer relationships and getting started that there is very little money coming in.

This brings up another point to remember: if you are a business owner and have employees, you may be paid the *most*, but you are also paid *last* after everyone else has been paid.

Long hours and isolation. Taking on a challenge as personal as developing your own business or beginning a professional practice can often be a lonely experience. You are following *your* dreams, *your* vision. Even those closest to you may not share it, or may not support it for that matter. As you work what will often be long hours, you may be alone much of the time. This is something you will have to get used to, at least for a while.

Busywork. Are you ready for a lot of paper work? Running a business requires much record keeping, even more so if you hire employees. Your time will be spent doing petty office tasks that do not feel connected to your mission, yet still have to be done.

Advantages

You have greater personal independence. Don't take that point too literally. You often do have greater flexibility in your scheduling, but there will always be limits.

When you run your own business and are serving customers, patients or clients, your schedule must first accommodate *their* needs. Many entrepreneurs are not necessarily their own bosses; they have several bosses: One boss in each and every customer, client or patient.

But let's look at the alternative: a typical company job. In this type of employment, you are normally accountable to your boss for a set number of hours each day. In some work environments, this commitment can be very difficult when personal issues or crises occur, such as a family illness or other emergency.

If you have your own business, you run your schedule, and you can better accommodate all the roles in your life.

There is greater personal gratification. This is true only if you answered the question of what you really care about. If you are pursuing a line of work which suits your talents and interests, is meaningful to you and adds to the quality of life for other people, then you will have deep feelings of satisfaction.

There is often greater financial reward. Most entrepreneurs will tell you that success does not happen overnight. Many who strike out on their own go through initial periods (months, perhaps years) where their profits and income are very low. But their objectives are *long-term*. When the payoff comes—and that normally happens gradually—it is often a pretty good one.

Is Starting a Business Right for You?

If the notion of starting a business doesn't thrill you, don't sweat it. It's not for everyone. But it is becoming the choice of more and more people every year. All I want you to know is that there is nothing to stop you from doing what you really want to do, TODAY.

Being paid for what you like to do has nothing to do with someone offering you a job. *It is what you can offer someone else.* If you can help them, you've met a need.

When you succeed at this even to the smallest degree, congratulations.

You have just given yourself a job.

What Next? Here Are Some Steps You Can Take Today

1) Begin the process of *Opportunity Recognition*. Ask yourself what kind of skill, hobby or work you find most rewarding and at which you have true talent. What kind of *need* do you feel your talent has the capacity to fill? Next, look to the marketplace, whether it is your community or the whole world.

Who else is also providing for that need, if at all? How are they doing it? How are they marketing it? How might you do it differently and better?

2) Talk to those in your network who are entrepreneurs and work closely with them. Find out their opinions and experiences. In chapter 8, you learned about SCORE, the Service Corps of Retired Executives. Give your local chapter a call and arrange a personal consultation. This is a free service that can be worth so much to your future. You have nothing to lose and everything to gain.

3) Check out "idea" books in your library, including those mentioned in this book. Also, be sure to read up on other issues regarding small business management, and focus especially on marketing and sales. After all, without sales, you won't have a business!

4) Decide what your goals will be. Once you have a destination, you need a road map to get you there. Clearly begin the process of setting tangible objectives, and construct a plan for reaching those objectives. This applies whether you are trying to start a small part-time enterprise or a full-time entrepreneurial career.

5) If you know what you want to do, find your first customer or client. Of course, the process of prospecting for him or her is not entirely different from that of finding an employer: you start with your network—the people who know you.

Getting Noticed:
An Idea Jogger to
Help You Stand Out

"I feel that it is vital to take on opportunities for leadership. It may not sound related to finding a good job, but it is very important. You have to learn to work with people, listen to them and also enforce the rules when necessary. It strengthens your integrity. What's more important than integrity?"

- William Matthews
  The University of Findlay
  Environmental and Hazardous
  Materials Management

As a child, William Matthews, a native of New Haven, Connecticut, knew that he wanted to dedicate his talents to preserving our planet.

"It first hit me when I went fishing as a kid," William recalls. "I caught a large bluefish that had apparently suffered from swimming in heavily polluted waters. It had a terrible odor and obviously was not safe to eat."

Since then, William has pursued a career in environmental and hazardous materials management, and he built this career using more than just his education.

During his high school days, William was involved in environmental research in one capacity or another. "From my junior year of high school, when I worked part-time as a research assistant, I had begun to develop a keen awareness of toxic materials and the damage they can do if they are not disposed of properly. I have done quite a bit of work in research, which has given me plenty of lab and field experience," William says.

By the time he was a junior in college, William, a multiple scholarship recipient, had done work in household waste disposal with the Yale University School of Medicine, and had learned to detect Lyme disease in ticks at the Connecticut Agricultural Experiment Station. William learned about these opportunities through contacts he made while in high school.

In addition to his part-time research work, William also contributed his time to his college as a resident assistant. "I feel that it is vital to take on opportunities for leadership. It may not sound related to finding a good job, but it is very important. You have to learn to work with people, listen to them and also enforce the rules when necessary. It strengthens your integrity. What's more important than integrity?"

In all of these pursuits, William has nurtured the deep motivation he has to improve the world, while at the same time advancing his own career. He has, through his work and service, kept his name and face in front of people. His many accomplishments became especially well-known when the University of Findlay selected William to be profiled and photographed in a brochure produced for the university's capital campaign.

As he prepares confidently for his job search, William has approached his career development from a different perspective. Rather than seeing himself as a student planning to go into a job of hazardous materials management, William has always viewed himself as an environmental advocate. His education and degree are two stages in playing that role, as he strives to take his contribution to a higher level and learns how to preserve our world.

Self Promotion

William's work during high school and college serve as an example of the points we have stressed all along. In order to begin developing a successful future career, you need to develop relationships, communication skills, experience, service and a work ethic. Furthermore, although William is dedicated to the greater good, he has also learned to take advantage of opportunities for self-advancement. The two ideas are not in opposition; rather, they are complimentary.

Up to this point, we have talked about the steps you must take to get a jump-start on your career while still in school, so that you aren't left wondering what to do the day after you graduate. When you need your first full-time job, think about these points we have stressed all along. And now, learn how to take them one step further.

In the introduction, I told you that I would not be discussing how to write a resume. To a certain extent, this is not completely true. Indeed, if you have been exercising the strategies in this book, you have actually been writing your resume as you went along.

More accurately, your resume has been writing itself.

However, the importance of the actual techniques of resume writing is greatly diminished when the central product—**you**—is more thoroughly developed, with a reputation that precedes itself. Let's face it, while resumes are important, they don't get jobs or build businesses, nor can you expect them to. **You** must get the jobs, not a piece of paper.

Much of what I have been discussing also relates strongly to gaining a better means of self-promotion. You must put yourself out into the world to build experience and relationships and to be in the right place at the right time. Even more, to help yourself professionally, you must get the word out about who you are, what you stand for and what you can do for others.

Why Now?

It works best the earlier you start. So once again, *don't wait until you graduate.* Self-promotion should become a habit that you will continue long after completing school.

Like relationship building, self-promotion has long-term goals. It is not something that can be accomplished overnight. Even though we live in a time when people must toot their own horns to become noticed, far too many people still fail to promote themselves, or they don't start until it is too late.

"Too late" is defined in two ways: being let go from a previous job or finishing school with no job waiting. Both scenarios leave the individual searching for work. And at that point, it is very difficult to begin promoting oneself.

People already in the work place fail to promote themselves for several reasons. The most prevalent is that they don't feel compelling needs to change jobs. It's an attitude of complacency, which sometimes comes from the illusion of job security or from plain, old procrastination. A person who has been with one corporation or organization for years and is viewed by himself and others as an integral part of the company is usually not thinking about being laid off. He probably is not going to put in the extra time and effort it takes to promote himself. That's the case until the last thing he is expecting occurs—he is let go.

Suddenly, he is scrambling in a panic.

He must update his resume.

He must start making phone calls.

He must see if anyone owes him any favors.

He must lose weight, get a haircut and buy a new suit.

And he must really look at his past service and make a list of what his major achievements were for his former company.

Complacency is your biggest enemy. There is no such thing today as complete job security. Businesses are bought and sold. Organizations lose their funding.

Students who are complacent often think they need only concentrate on their studies and activities and that the future will take care of itself. Early on in my college career I remember being told that all activities are second only to studying and getting good grades. If studies take up all my time, I was told, then so be it.

Deep down, I never agreed with that philosophy. I think a C student who is a great friend to people, a strong self-promoter and is dedicated to serving others and the community may go much further than an A student who does nothing else but attend class and score high on examinations.

The lesson here is actually twofold. The rule of self-promotion while you are in school is don't wait until you graduate. Once you get a job after graduation, the rule is don't wait until you get fired!

Self-Promotion and Marketing

If your course of study is not business-related, then you may not have had any exposure to basic marketing principles. This is a shame, because everyone needs to be a salesperson to get ahead. Everyone must know how to market himself or herself.

Some marketing basics:

Let's quickly review some of the key elements of successful marketing and later explain how they relate to your self-promotion. There are four key elements necessary for marketing success.

1. Product benefits

One of the biggest mistakes people make in marketing is to emphasize the product rather than the benefits it provides. Whether you are selling a product or a service, what you are truly selling are benefits. Think about the following items, and ask yourself why you may or may not have them:

- Toothpaste
- A car
- A magazine subscription
- Cable television
- A music library
- A computer
- A favorite restaurant

It really makes a difference to look at yourself and your own list of skills the same way you might look at this list of products above.

What specific benefits do people or organizations need that you have the capacity to provide, either now or in the future? Based on your own list, do you think employers would want you?

2. A clearly defined audience

Another thing to think about when looking at product benefits is how the products themselves are positioned. That is, the sales pitch for certain similar products is often directed at different audiences through different messages.

The way cars are marketed serves as a prime example. Look at how car companies pitch their automobiles to various audiences. Would you sell a Mazda Miata the same way you would sell a Dodge Caravan or a Ford Escort? Of course not. While all three cars deliver the same benefit of transportation, they do so in different ways for different people with different interests.

When you enter the job search, it's not enough to know yourself and what you can do. You must also know whom you are talking to and who you can help. You must know what these people's concerns are, as well as their problems and their values.

From a career jump-starting perspective, defining your audience works very much in your favor. I remember a close friend telling me a story about the time a large corporation came to his college campus to interview college seniors. Hundreds of students showed up. The interviewers reduced the crowd instantly by asking all students with a GPA of less than 3.5 to go home.

Good news! Many of today's smaller companies and organizations are being run by people more interested in bottom-line objectives than restrictions, company rules and blanket policies and procedures. So what if you didn't qualify to talk with the larger company which had the GPA requirement? Maybe this company was not the right audience for you. Chances are, you can find other, more receptive audiences in small company managers and entrepreneurs. Typically, they aren't nearly as concerned about your grades as they are about how you can help their companies succeed. If you can promote yourself and your abilities successfully, then you can show them that you have the qualities they want.

These are the things you must think about when evaluating your audience. Are you seeking employment from a big corporation, a medium-sized company or a small business? What are these employers looking for? What do they want? What can you give them? How will you tell them? This leads us to the next point:

3. A consistent message

Most marketing experts will agree that consistency is a key element in long-term marketing success. This includes consistency in image and consistency in message.

Consistency in message is a prime focus here. To really get the word out on a product, you have to hammer away at it. You have to hit your audience with your message over and over again until they really begin to respond. One-shot deals don't cut it. It doesn't help to throw one message out, and if people don't respond instantly, to switch to another.

Selling yourself is no exception. However, deciding on a message for yourself can be difficult when jump-starting your career, especially if you don't know what you wish to do with your life yet.

So while a consistent message is important, it may take some time to develop one. Until then, here's a tidbit that might put your heart at ease: concentrate on promoting your name.

Half the game of self-promotion is keeping yourself in front of people. As you progress in your education and career development, you may change majors, interests, residences and schools. But your name remains a symbol of yourself.

Of course, some women and even men change their names when they marry. So if you decide to change your name, be sure to telegraph the news and make the connection clear.

As a general rule, it's a good idea to get some stationery custom-printed with your name on it. There are several mail-order houses that offer stationery at a low price, and most print shops can do the same. Start treating your name like a trademark. Later on, you will learn additional ways to use your name and keep it in front of people.

4. A convenient means of response (you must be accessible)

Ever notice how when a magazine solicits a subscription from you, they always have a postage-paid, business-reply envelope enclosed? They can't afford to lose an order just because someone can't find a stamp.

How about mail-order ads you see in print and on television? Almost all have toll-free numbers where you can dial in and use your credit card to order. It reduces sales if customers must go through the hassle of copying an address, sitting down to write a check as well as having to put the order in the mail.

Now you may think, *Well, that's no big deal. An employer who's interested can just call me.* And you are right. If you can be reached easily by phone and you have an answering machine, you are in pretty good shape. If you can also be notified by mail, even better.

However, your phone number and address may change often while you are in school. Some students find themselves moving to new addresses almost every year. Other students have roommates who are not reliable at taking messages, either from a person or an answering machine.

This hinders your ability to be contacted by potential employers. It also sets you up for great embarrassment.

Here is where both consistency and accessibility come into play. I know some people who move often, and quite frankly, it's annoying when I look in my address book and wonder if I have the correct information. Might people have that problem with you?

Here are some solutions: a post office box, voice mail and E-mail.

If you are not planning to be at your physical address for at least the next two years, go to the local post office (where the prices are the lowest) and apply for a small P.O. box. My box only costs $40 per year and has allowed me to keep the same mailing address, even though I have moved three times since obtaining it.

Voice mail is another option. It costs just a little more— about $10 per month—but the phone number will not change if you move. If you wish, you can forward calls from your home phone to that number or simply tell people to call it directly, twenty-four hours a day. When leaving phone messages for people whom you want to call you back, don't even waste your time relying on roommates or family members. Get your own private voice mail service.

The greeting on your voice mail should be short and professional. Since the caller may be limited in his or her message time, politely tell the person that how long he or she has to leave a message and phone number, and that you will get back to them as quickly as possible.

If you move a lot or have irresponsible roommates, consider these two options. If you have a computer, you should make use of E-mail and the Internet. Most colleges and universities automatically supply their students with e-mail addresses. If you're not sure whether you have one or not, check with your college to find out. Also, ask where the computer labs are located. These are sites that the college maintains where computers are available to students for personal and school use. If you have a personal computer at home or in your dorm room, you should be able to use your campus e-mail address there as well.

Another resource to check out is the local "free-Net." In my community, the free-Net is funded by Ohio State University and other private donors and businesses. All you need to access it is a public library card. The free-Net provides access to databases and networks all over the world and allows you to send and receive E-mail, all for the cost of a local phone call.

Once you have Internet access, another option is to obtain a free e-mail address through one of the many Internet sites that provide that service (hotmail, yahoo, etc.). Even if you have an e-mail address through school or a commercial service, you may want to utilize one of free services to get a second e-mail address which sounds more professional than your personal account. For example, if your e-mail address is something like Happybunny123@aol.com or cooldude85@mind-spring.com, it would certainly be to your advantage to have an e-mail address like JaneSmith@hotmail.com or JTSmith@yahoo.com.

Once you obtain an Internet address, be sure to place it on all of your correspondence so that people will know how to reach you via E-mail. Perhaps more importantly, you must *use* your e-mail and *check it regularly*. It won't do you much good if you rarely check it or don't respond to others' messages promptly.

Your personal stationery should now include all of the following items:

- Your full name

- Your full mailing address (or post office box if you move every one or two years)
- Your home phone number
- Your twenty-four-hour voice mail number (if you have room-mates or children who answer the phone)
- Your E-mail address

If you follow these steps, people who see a letter or even a business card from you will have a positive first impression that you take yourself seriously and really have it together. They will also appreciate the convenience you offer them of easily being able to get in touch with you.

Just remember to check messages regularly and answer them promptly. All this access to you is meaningless if you don't!

How These Lessons Apply to Your Self-Promotion

As I said before, half the game of self-promotion is keeping your name in front of people. You are the product. When you adopt the habit of promoting yourself, you are constantly seeking opportunities for people to see you, hear you, read your name and eventually want to hire you.

Sound intimidating? Many of you may think so; others of you may think not. It can be tough for a person just starting a career to hype him or herself. Indeed, even more so if you are not sure what you may want to do with your life.

But relax, I know you can do it. Think about all the skills you have learned and accomplished already.

Your Top Priority

In earlier chapters, we talked about how volunteer and paid work allow you to demonstrate your skills, your character and your work ethic. By working, you are promoting yourself. You are allowing your name to become associated with the character and quality of service you exemplify.

It is this association that you want most. At this point, it makes no real difference whether you wish to pursue a career in auto repair, law, medicine, social service or education. All the degrees and skills in the world can't help you if you don't have the credibility and respect of your peers. If people do not perceive you as someone of integrity and character, with a strong work ethic, how can you expect them to hire you?

So make developing your character your first objective. A good name and reputation among others will soon follow.

Many of the suggestions, or idea joggers, in the previous and upcoming pages should be considered. Take the next step; then all the rest will be easier to undertake.

Some Helpful Ideas to Promote Yourself and Make Yourself More Promotable
Be a Problem Solver

So far, you have learned about opportunities in both the non-profit sector and in business. In all cases, you have been faced with two objectives:

1) Becoming a solution to a problem.

2) Being there when someone needs you.

What would you rather list on your resume of life: a string of jobs or a track record of accomplishments? There are plenty of challenges and opportunities to accomplish great things all around you. Keep your eyes open. And remember, *A job can be taken away from you; an accomplishment cannot.*

This is why you must not be afraid to take on challenges and create them for yourself. There are organizations that need help in order to accomplish their missions. There are companies and entrepreneurs who wish to increase sales and profits. If you can make people's lives easier or better, your achievements will make you stand head and shoulders above the rest.

Seek Work that Allows You to Interact with Others

You read about many opportunities in previous chapters on volunteering, internships, service learning and summer employment. It is easy to settle for some quiet occupation that keeps you in a closed office all day. You might prefer that environment in working hours, but don't let it dominate your life!

If you find a job or volunteer in a professional organization, get involved in that organization's public relations efforts. That could mean doing phone work or planning events. It may even include newsletter writing. Either way, it offers you the chance to keep your face, and your name, in front of many people.

Public relations is a great means of learning the art of promotion. Even if you aren't studying it for a career, it will help you tremendously to have practical experience in it, so you can apply what you've learned to promote yourself.

Practice an "Elevator Drill"

The "elevator drill" is an exercise you practice which allows you to explain what you do in the length of time it takes for an elevator door to close. It means condensing your most valuable qualities and services into twenty-five to forty words.

Then, if someone asks, "What do you do?" or "What are you studying?" you have a quick answer ready.

Of course, you may be undecided about your career. But this is not a problem. If you are following the advice in this book, you should still have something to talk about. Place what you do in the context of *what you're doing today*, as opposed to what you think you might do in the future.

Explaining yourself in this way might not always be easy; and keeping it short can also be a challenge. There may be much more you want to say. The good part is that if your listener is genuinely interested and has a few moments, he will ask for more information.

So talk about what you are doing now, be it volunteer work, Service Learning or a summer job. Relate it, if you can, to what you are studying. Get excited. Show enthusiasm!

If You Can't Write Well, Learn How

Having good communication skills is very important to potential employers. We have already documented that. You will probably need to be able to write letters, proposals or other documents once you get a job. But, you also need good writing skills for when you write a letter to a prospective employer to request a summer job, or when you write to an organization with a suggestion to design your own internship. If your material is poorly written, the employer will gain an equally poor impression of you and your abilities.

Writing is not easy. Even professional writers have to keep their skills polished. In fact, as I read through the first drafts of this book, often I came across an awkward sentence or something out of place that made me think, *Now that's not what I meant to convey!* Rethinking, reformulating and rewriting are part of the process of expressing what you mean as succinctly as possible.

Here are a few ways to work on your writing skills:

1. Don't blow off your English requirement.

We all have had some classes in school that we were required to take and would never have enrolled in on our own. In such classes, it often takes real effort to put our hearts into studying and doing the work. I remember many students in my college treating the study of English composition this way.

Writing in one form or another is germane to most careers. There will be papers, proposals, notes and letters which you will need to compose. Pay particular attention to English and writing classes even if you are not inclined to do so on your own.

Look to your instructors as writing coaches. Find out from them what parts of your writing need work. If there is a part of writing which tends to trouble you more than others, seek their advice on overcoming it. Remember, you are paying them to help you. Get your money's worth!

2. Write for your school newspaper or local newsletters.

Whether you have an interest in journalism or not, try writing for your schools' newspaper. I was surprised to find when I started writing for the *Ohio State Lantern* that virtually anyone on campus who was willing to make a commitment and could produce decent copy could be published in the newspaper. Being a reporter wasn't restricted to journalism students.

At Ohio State we had many students writing their own columns in the *Lantern* each quarter. Again, they weren't all journalism majors, nor were they all upperclassmen. These were students who were willing to make modest commitments to express their views on different subjects.

Our newspaper also had paid reporter positions, for those students (mostly from the news-editorial department) interested in gaining writing and reporting experience. These jobs also provided great ways to help students become better-known throughout the campus community.

Local newsletters, particularly for non-profit organizations, also offer tremendous opportunities to accumulate writing experience and to get your name in front of people. The newsletter which I edit is written mostly by volunteers. It goes out to business and community leaders as well as to religious organizations. Believe me, many groups and organizations would be eager to offer you the chance to help them out.

There are many other benefits to writing for school or local newsletters. You will learn how to gather facts and information and how to package them for a particular audience. This will build better research skills and improve the way you write. This will also give you access to people, opportunities and information which can help your career.

3. Keep a journal.

This is one of the most recommended ways to improve your writing skills—and it is often the most difficult. Chances are your English teacher will encourage you to write a personal journal and perhaps make it an ongoing class assignment.

Keeping a journal requires discipline and concentration, even if you are only writing a few words per day. In today's noisy and hectic world, finding the needed peace and quiet can be a real challenge.

However, it is worth the trouble. A private journal will help you improve your writing in ways other methods may not. While writing for a newsletter requires looking outside of yourself, journal writing requires looking within. When you write in a journal, you are expressing your personal feelings and thoughts about events in your life, your daily activities and your relationships.

Keeping a journal is also a great way to put your life in perspective. It helps you remain accountable to yourself, especially if you, like many people, have a tendency to start many things without seeing them through to the end.

Write a journal for six months to a year, or even longer; then read it from the beginning. You may be surprised at how your life, your priorities and your relationships evolve over time (and how your writing has improved!). You may be even more astonished to see how your journal-keeping has affected your ability to stay on track—to get you from where you were to where you wanted to be. You can also record all of your accomplishments as they happen. Then, when it's time to write or update your resume, you can look back through your journal to remind yourself of all that you have done.

If you decide to keep a journal, you can make entries as often as you like. I recommend writing often—daily if possible, but certainly at least a couple times a week—so that it becomes a habit. Otherwise, before you know it, six months have gone by and your journal will be full of blank pages.

If You Can't Speak Well to an Audience, Learn How

This skill goes hand-in-hand with writing, both of which comprise part of your overall ability to communicate effectively. Public speaking is something which does not come naturally to many people and can be most intimidating.

However, being able to speak and express yourself effectively will greatly enhance your self-promotion. Employers seek individuals with excellent presentation skills. If you can demonstrate those skills, you are bound to make a great impression and give yourself an advantage.

Why is presentation so important, even if you aren't working in sales or some other position where you interact with a lot of people?

Look at it this way: when you work for an organization or institution, either as an employee or a volunteer, you are their representative. When you speak on behalf of a larger group, people's impressions of that group will be based upon their impression of you.

The same is true if you have started your own business, as we discussed in the previous chapter. How well you are able to pitch your abilities to a prospective client will make a big difference to your business. If you promote yourself poorly, you soon won't have a business to promote at all!

If you would like the opportunity to practice your public speaking skills, I have two suggestions: Toastmasters and volunteering. Toastmasters International is an organization that provides a supportive, positive and fun environment in which to increase your skill and confidence in thinking, speaking, listening and leadership. Most chapters offer a self-paced step-by-step program with educational manuals. If public speaking is something you have had little opportunity to try, consider taking this type of a course.

Or, if you have a knack for speaking and would like to practice a bit more, then I would urge you to volunteer. Many community groups seek people to speak to their constituents on their behalf. This helps the group to build visibility and spread their news by word of mouth, and it also increases your own visibility. In fact, presentations are a big part of fund-raising campaigns and are most often done by volunteers.

Once you begin to develop professionally, speaking well and often to small and large groups will help you progress toward your career goals.

Keep a Portfolio of Your Accomplishments

Involved in a project or an event that was featured in the local paper? Cut out the clipping and highlight the actual benefit it provided to that organization or the community. If it was on television, keep a videotape copy on hand.

Have you ever gotten a thank you letter, or a note commending you for a job well done? Keep them! Make plenty of copies, and store them in a safe place.

Have you successfully helped create or market a new product or service? Collect samples of the printed materials involved, with documentation of the results.

Anything you can show people that reflects contributions on your part should be kept and made part of your collection. Take the clippings, letters and printed materials and place them in clear plastic sleeves which fit in a small three-ring binder. Don't use anything flashy or expensive. Just something that documents the contribution you have made to other people's lives or businesses.

You may be surprised at the great reception your collection gets.

What Next? Here Are Some Steps You Can Take Today

1) Begin a resume file. Here, you will collect items which document all the accomplishments you will want to list on your resume. You will soon collect several folders for your file. There will be one for each subject area such as school activities, volunteer work, professional associations, employment, etc. Remember to include a folder for thank you letters and other acknowledgments.

2) Be accessible. If your circumstances require it, get yourself the following: a post office box, voice mail and definitely E-mail. Have all of this information available on your own stationery and business cards.

3) We talked about the importance of interacting with others. Sales work can be a wonderful opportunity to do this and to learn about the process in general. You will also learn about sales from people you meet who are involved in it. This can be someone with whom you work or volunteer. Remember, organizations of all kinds use sales people, even non-profit organizations.

If you have the opportunity to do public relations work or even to do "selling" of some sort for your employer or other volunteer organization, respond to it. We are all selling a product, and ultimately that product is ourselves.

In appendix III, you will read about a book called *Relationship Selling*. I strongly recommend that you get a copy of this book and read it.

4) Get started writing. It is amazing how many people come out of college and cannot write. Write for your school paper. Write for professional association newsletters. (They need the copy!) Your writing will improve and not only will your articles get in front of people, so will your name!

5) Attend a Toastmasters meeting or explore other opportunities to work on speaking and presentation skills. If public speaking is your greatest fear, all the more reason to start doing it now. Don't wait!

Conclusion

What Goes Around, Comes Around

When I began writing this book, newspaper headlines announced that job prospects for new college graduates were dismal. By the time the first edition of this book was published, the economy had improved considerably. The headlines said that job prospects for college graduates had improved—so long as the career being sought was in an industry experiencing growth or a sector with a high demand for employees. Today, the economic situation has worsened again and the news is out: job prospects are once again poor. The most important message of these headlines is that conditions fluctuate. These variations reinforce several facts:

- Economic ups and downs will continue.
- The concept of the one-company, cradle-to-grave employer is long gone.

Most experts concur that in today's world, a career is not usually a straight climb up a ladder. Rather, a career will most likely be a zigzag path in which a person builds skills and seasoning from one opportunity or job, and applies them to another. As one's personal experience and expertise increase, most likely, so will the level of these opportunities.

Because we live in an era of rapid technological, economic and social change, college students of today and tomorrow will all face tough challenges, whatever their graduation day headlines read. Launching a career is one of the biggest. Because of this, you must not wait until you graduate to get started. You must be innovative and creative, and possess a dedication to benefiting others, in order to achieve long-term success and short-term victories. And you must begin today.

In the introduction to this book, we talked about "planting the seeds of your career" while in college, and letting them grow. These "seeds" are your character, your skills and your relationships.

In terms of the bottom-line impact, or benefit, as my introduction said:

Many job-hunt guides and manuals present a "road map" approach, promising results within a given period of time if you follow their specific steps.

But it's not that easy. Remember, the reality is that there exists a zigzagging path to a fulfilling career or to the job of your dreams. Success really occurs when you consistently apply fundamental principles and focus on serving others. Sooner or later, you achieve good results on which you can build a productive and rewarding future.

- You nurture the seeds of your character by being honest, and always striving for quality results.
- You nurture the seeds of your skills as you take classes and become involved in new experiences and try new things.
- You nurture the seeds of your relationships, widening your circle of intimates and friends by getting to know other people and getting other people to know you.

Can you expect to do any of these things quickly? No more so than a hungry man who plants tomato seeds in the morning can expect to eat tomatoes later that evening.

I would like to relate one interesting observation made by researchers at the University of California, Los Angeles. At the Cooperative Institutional Research Program, they have conducted surveys of college freshmen over the last thirty years. One recurring issue that the surveys looked into has been students' personal values in having a "philosophy of life" versus "earning a living."[1] The presumption seems to be that these are separate entities. I believe that this is a faulty presumption. Why is it assumed that these two values contradict each other? Does it suggest that people who earn good livings have sold their souls to the devil?

I think this is mostly not the case. After all, our nation is responsible for most of the advances in the twentieth century, largely because people were motivated by rewards for their achievements. But these achievements continue to improve and better our lives to this very day. And many of the people who have invented or contributed to them have strong spiritual values as well.

Further, it pleases me to see that today's younger generation has placed a renewed focus on community service. Experts have named Generation Y as "the most socially conscious generation since the '60s."[2] Throughout their grade school, high school and college years, young people today are volunteering in record numbers.

I hope that after finishing these chapters, you do not come away from this book with the attitude that I am giving you yet "another thing to do" in your busy schedule. Rather, I hope you will gain knowledge of an important strategy for your future:

- A **clear understanding** that there are plenty of small steps which you can take today that can have a huge impact on your life tomorrow
- **Peace of mind** in knowing that opportunities for you, in the form of needs, exist everywhere
- **Reassurance** in that networking is not just another game of cold-calling and business card passing, but a process of building relationships

I also hope you will develop a new **self understanding**. Many people view themselves only in terms of "earning capacity." Sure, your earnings are important. But remember, others will not view you in terms of what you will take from the table, but in what you will bring to it. The rewards we earn in life, be they material, emotional or spiritual, are often parallel to the impact we make on the lives of others. Ask yourself the question, "What impact can I have?"

An experience I recently had exemplifies these points very well. Part of my work fundraising for non-profit organizations involves interviewing people. Last year, I had the opportunity to interview the head of a hospital in northern Pennsylvania. One comment he made cut to the real issue, not only in health care, but in the essence of work for us all:

"With all this talk about the financing and economics of healthcare, the real issue I think still boils down to the *quality of service* itself. If we lose focus on caring for the needs of patients, if we lose focus on making a contribution to the quality of life for the people in our community, then it won't matter how strong we are financially, because eventually we will lose that too."

Earnings are important. Profit is not a dirty word, regardless of whether you choose to enter a non-profit or commercial field. But the real goal is to satisfy a need and provide a true benefit to someone else.

You have heard the expression, "What goes around, comes around." I have heard it used to describe the consequences of immoral or dishonest behavior. But it applies equally to positive work.

- Your commitment to helping others honestly (character) will determine the quality of your service.
- The quality of your service (skills) will determine the quality of your relationships.
- The quality of your relationships will determine the quality of your opportunities.
- The quality of your opportunities, and the commitment with which you respond to them, will determine your own quality of life.

In today's changing global economy, tomorrow's leaders and citizens must learn to see themselves not merely in terms of how much they can earn, but in how their talents can be used to benefit others. They must understand that while it is nobody's obligation to employ them, it is their social responsibility to provide for themselves by providing for their communities, their country and the world.

The end result is this: if you adopt the philosophy described in this book, if you **don't wait until you graduate** to begin working and servicing needs of businesses, institutions and communities, and building relationships with other people, you will succeed.

Follow the steps I have outlined in this book, and your career will have begun before you know it. You will plant the seeds for your career *before* you graduate. Will it lead to stronger relationships and better experience? Definitely. Will it lead to a first job? Quite possibly...

I have no doubt that **it will happen** for many of you.

Appendix I

Organizations that Need Your Help

What follows is merely a sampling of nationally based non-profit organizations that thrive due to the support of volunteers. While I mainly listed those which had branches and/or chapters in cities across the country, you should not regard this list as totally comprehensive. For additional sources of information, check in appendix III.

Blanket Organizations

These are organizations which serve other non-profits through the supply of interested volunteers. If you have certain skills or interests, these are good places to start looking for opportunities.

USA Freedom Corps.
1600 Pennsylvania Avenue, NW
Washington, DC 20500
Telephone: 877-872-2677
E-mail: Info@usafreedomcorps.gov
Website: http://www.usafreedomcorps.org

President George W. Bush has called on all Americans to commit at least 4,000 hours—the equivalent of two years—over the course of their lives to the service of others. To help facilitate this vision, the USA Freedom Corps Network allows individuals to find service opportunities that match their interests and talents in their hometowns, across the country or around the world. New opportunities are emerging in homeland security, extending American compassion around the world through our volunteer service infrastructure (which include the Peace Corps, Citizen Corps, AmeriCorps and Senior Corps). It also raises awareness of and breaks down barriers to service opportunities with all federal government agencies.

Corporation for National and Community Service
Learn and Serve America
1201 New York Avenue, NW
Washington, DC 20525
Telephone: 202-606-5000
Website: http://www.nationalservice.org

Through service-learning programs supported by the Corporation for National and Community Service (CNCS), over a million and a half students from kindergarten through higher education apply academic skills to solve real needs in over 3,000 local communities. In schools, colleges and community organizations, young people improve their studies, develop problem-solving skills and incorporate the habits of good citizenship while improving their communities.

CNCS has the National Service-Learning Clearinghouse that can be reached by telephone at 866-245-SERV (7378) or on the web at www.servicelearning.org. They also offer training and technical assistance through the Learn and Serve America Training and Technical Assistance Exchange, which can be reached toll-free at 877-LSA-EXCH (877-572-3924) or on the web at www.nslexchange.org.

Further, the CNCS website offers a wealth of information on AmeriCorps and the National Senior Service Corps, as well as the new USA Freedom Corps. In addition, there are state level contacts for all programs.

CNCS also supports three awards programs that are available to all Americans and their communities: Presidential Freedom Scholarships,

President's Student Service Awards and National Service-Learning Leader School Recognition.

Presidential Freedom Scholarships: Each high school in the country may select two junior or senior year students to receive a $1,000 scholarship for outstanding service to the community. CNCS provides $500 for each scholarship matched with $500 from the community. Scholarship recipients must have served at least 100 hours in their communities within a twelve month period. In addition to the scholarship, students receive the President's Student Service Award gold pin, as well as a presidential certificate. For more information, visit their website: www.nationalservice.org/scholarships.

President's Student Service Awards: Students who contribute at least 100 hours of service to the community in a twelve month period are eligible for the President's Student Service Award. Students may be certified by schools, colleges or community organizations and will receive a specially designed gold pin with the presidential seal, and a presidential certificate. Youth ages five to fourteen who perform fifty hours of community service within a twelve month period may receive a silver pin with the presidential seal, as well as a presidential certificate. For more information, visit their website: www.student-service-awards.org.

National Service-Learning Leader Schools / Learn and Serve America sponsors an initiative to identify and recognize the top service-learning programs in middle and high schools across the nation. For more information about the National Service-Learning Leader Schools initiative visit their website: www.leaderschools.org.

ACCESS: Networking in the Public Interest
1001 Connecticut Avenue, NW
Suite 838
Washington, DC 20036
Telephone: 800-417-6351
Website: http://www.accessjobs.org

ACCESS is a national clearinghouse that provides information on internship and employment opportunities in community service.

Through its monthly publication, *Community Jobs*, ACCESS lists jobs and internship opportunities at non-profit and government agencies. ACCESS also publishes *The National Service Guide*, a comprehensive directory of service organizations and volunteer centers nationwide, as well as resources for finding employment in the non-profit sector.

Campus Outreach Opportunity League (COOL)

37 Temple Place
Suite 401
Boston, MA 02111
Telephone: 617-695-2665
E-mail: inquiry@cool2serve.org
Website: http://www.cool2serve.org

Founded in 1984, COOL is a national non-profit organization that helps college students start, strengthen and expand their community service programs. COOL works with hundreds of campuses and thousands of students. Its staff visits college campuses giving workshops to encourage, promote and initiate programs that get students involved in community service.

Independent Sector

1200 18th Street, NW
Suite 200
Washington, DC 20036
Telephone: 202-467-6100
E-mail: info@IndependentSector.org
Website: http://www.independentsector.org

Independent Sector is a coalition of nearly a thousand corporations, foundations and voluntary organizations dedicated to the advancement of philanthropy and voluntary service across the nation. This is the organization which initiated the "Give Five" campaign, urging everyone to dedicate just five hours per week or five percent of their income to a cause that was important to them. Independent Sector also distributes many publications and periodicals, conducts research and advocates for the non-profit sector in legislation battles.

Points of Light Foundation
1400 I Street, NW
Suite 800
Washington, DC 20005
Telephone: 202-729-8000 / 800-750-7653
E-mail: info@pointsoflight.org
Website: http://www.pointsoflight.org

The driving belief behind the Points of Light Foundation is that creative, proactive and catalytic volunteer centers are critical to increasing volunteerism in America today. The organization is committed to working in partnership with local Volunteer Centers to promote community service aimed at serious social problems. It also provides opportunities to work together on nationwide programs and assistance to Volunteer Centers in building public recognition and support through training and consultation.

The United Way of America
701 North Fairfax Street
Alexandria, VA 22314
Telephone: 703-836-7100
Website: http://www.unitedway.org

There are more than 2,300 independently incorporated, community-based United Way chapters throughout the country. Each United Way chapter offers support to local organizations serving various community needs. You can easily find your local United Way office by visiting the website, clicking on "Find My Local United Way" and entering your zip code. Then you can visit your local United Way office and browse their Agency Directory which lists the non-profit groups in your area supported by the United Way.

Social Service Organizations

Many of these organizations specialize in poverty, racial and child-related issues, and offer services to suit their individual communities. One thing is certain—demand for their services (and yours) is never lacking.

Alliance for Children and Families
11700 West Lake Park Drive
Milwaukee, WI 53224
Telephone: 414-359-1040 / 800-221-3726
Website: http://alliance1.org

Through nearly 350 non-profit member associations, the Alliance for Children and Families serves more than 5 million individuals in over 2,000 communities, providing a vast array of services to strengthen the building block of our society: families. These services range from dealing with marital difficulties to parent-child relationship tensions and eradicating drug abuse, child abuse and domestic violence. Volunteers are needed for support services, mentoring and child care.

American Red Cross
4310 18th Street, NW
Washington, DC 20006
Telephone: 202-639-3520 / 877-272-7337
Website: http://www.redcross.org

Most often when people think of the Red Cross, they think of blood donations and disaster relief. But the American Red Cross engages in many types of human service activities across the country, as well as in military installations abroad. Their 1.1 million volunteers support staff members through 2,700 chapters in health clinics, hospitals, collection centers and wherever help is needed.

Volunteers are in demand for counseling children and victims of disaster and for providing relief in time of emergencies. Local Red Cross chapters also utilize the services of other board and committee volunteers.

American Social Health Association
(National AIDS Hotline)
P.O. Box 13827
Research Triangle Park, NC 27709
Telephone: 919-361-8400 / 800-342-2437
Website: http://www.ashastd.org

The American Social Health Association (ASHA) operates the National AIDS Hotline, which provides callers with information regarding AIDS and related issues. ASHA aims to prevent the spread of social diseases through education and leadership. It also refers callers to local support services, such as public health clinics, volunteer centers, alternative HIV testing sights, counseling services and advocacy groups.

The ASPIRA Association, Inc.

1444 Eye Street, NW
Suite 800
Washington, DC 20005
Telephone: 202-835-3600
E-mail: info@aspira.org
Website: http://www.aspira.org

The ASPIRA Association, (the name comes from the Spanish verb aspirar, which means, to aspire to something greater), serves Puerto Rican and Latino youth through education and leadership development. While the organization only has twelve offices across the country, it does work through over 2,000 other community-based organizations to reach more than 13,000 children. Volunteer opportunities include mentoring, hospital work, counseling, working on food and clothing drives and providing support for the homeless.

The Association of Junior Leagues International Inc.

132 West 31st Street
11th Floor
New York, NY 10001-3406
Telephone: 212-951-8300
E-mail: info@ajli.org
Website: http://www.ajli.org

The Association of Junior Leagues, a women's organization, is an international group of women which encourages volunteerism and community action throughout the United States, Canada, Mexico and Great Britain. Their combined membership exceeds 170,000. Members have advocated and worked on behalf of such issues as substance abuse, child abuse and neglect, education, cultural enrichment and urban concerns.

Big Brothers/Big Sisters of America, Inc.
230 North 13th Street
Philadelphia, PA 19107
Telephone: 215-567-7000
E-mail: national@bbbsa.org
Website: http://www.bbbsa.org

Big Brothers/Big Sisters operates through nearly 500 branches nationwide to help young adults and children who lack a strong role model in their lives. Most of these children have only one parent, and are considered to be at-risk. When you volunteer, you are asked to commit four to six hours each week for a year. The commitment of time usually only involves quality time with the youngsters, like outings and trips to the park. Volunteers are carefully screened and then matched with children to ensure the best success for all people involved. Training and support is provided.

Tens of thousands of children are on their waiting list. So give your local chapter a call.

Boy Scouts of America, National Council
1325 Walnut Hill Lane
P.O. Box 152079
Irving, TX 75015
Telephone: 214-580-2000
Website: http://www.scouting.org

The Boy Scouts aim to build character within our nation's boys. It does this through instilling a sense of civil and social responsibility, self-reliance and physical fitness. Not only do Boy Scouts provide tremendous services to their communities as part of their programs, but they are one of the biggest volunteer organizations in the country, with over a million people involved.

These men and women serve as chairpersons, group leaders and coordinators. Do you have expertise in a particular subject? You could become an authorized volunteer to approve merit badges on that subject.

Boys and Girls Clubs of America
1230 West Peachtree Street, NW
Atlanta, GA 30309
Telephone: 404-487-5700
Website: http://www.bgca.org

The Boys and Girls Clubs of America aim to positively influence young people at a time when that influence is most critical. This includes building self-esteem, providing kids with good models and instilling positive values. It is the only non-profit organization of its kind that specifically targets disadvantaged children. The organization's 600 local clubs are professionally staffed, with daytime and after school programs in areas including athletics and fitness, job skills, drug abuse prevention and health care. Their branches tend to respond to specific community needs and offer a wide variety of service opportunities.

Camp Fire USA
4601 Madison Avenue
Kansas City, MO 64112
Telephone: 816-756-1950
Website: http://www.campfire.org

Camp Fire serves more than a half million children across the United States, from infancy to age twenty-one. It reaches them through four basic areas: clubs, camping programs, self-reliance courses and child care. Much of the organization's effectiveness in service, accomplished through informal and experiential education, is drawn from the very people it serves. Members learn the meaning of becoming responsible, caring, self-directed individuals. They run food programs, and work to prevent crime, teen suicide, drug abuse and promiscuity. Volunteer opportunities vary widely from chapter to chapter.

Child Welfare League of America
Headquarters
440 First Street, NW
3rd Floor
Washington, DC 20001-2085
Program Office
50 F Street, NW
6th Floor
Washington, DC 20001-2085
Telephone: 202-638-2952
Website: http://www.cwla.org

The Child Welfare League of America is dedicated to protecting and promoting the well-being of troubled children. It plays an important role in setting international standards and legislation regarding adoption, child care, child abuse, neglect, child protective services and foster care.

Children's Rights of America, Inc.
12551 Indian Rocks Road
Suite 9
Largo, FL 34644
Telephone: 813-593-0090
Youth Crisis Hotline: 800-442-4673
Hotline for parents and law officials: 800-874-1111

Children who have run away have often been abused or abandoned, become destitute or homeless, and in some cases, turn to drugs or prostitution. The CRA collects and distributes accurate statistics on missing and abused or exploited children. It also advocates on behalf of runaway teens, and educates the public on similar issues.

Family Promise (formerly National Interfaith Hospitality Networks)
71 Summit Avenue
Summit, NJ 07901
Telephone: 908-273-1100
Email: info@nihn.org
Website: http://www.nihn.org and http://www.familypromise.org

Regarded as a community response to homeless families, Family Promise works in cities all over the country utilizing each city's existing resources such as religious congregations of all denominations and their houses of worship. Volunteers in these congregations provide shelter, meals and compassionate assistance. Over 70 percent of families who participate in Family Promise programs find permanent housing; and guests who are jobless often acquire permanent employment or enter job training programs. If your congregation is not a participant of Family Promise, call the number listed.

Girl Scouts of the USA
420 Fifth Avenue
New York, NY 10018-2798
Telephone: 212-852-8000 / 800-478-7248
Website: http://www.girlscouts.org

Membership in the Girl Scouts include more than 2.2 million girls ages five to seventeen, and nearly 700,000 adults (both women and men). The Girl Scouts helps each girl reach her full potential through such activities as career exploration and community service. Girls are introduced to the arts, sciences and the environment. The organization also stresses the importance of working with people and building relationships.

Goodwill Industries of America, Inc.
9200 Rockville Pike
Bethesda, MD 20814
Telephone: 240-333-5200
E-mail: contactus@goodwill.org
Website: http://www.goodwill.org

Goodwill is much more than a donation collection center and a chain of thrift stores. It also provides physically, mentally or economically disabled individuals with training, support and counseling to become productive members of society. Volunteer and career opportunities exist at all levels. Many Goodwill chapters around the country, in fulfilling their entrepreneurial tradition, provide a vast array of services for their communities.

Habitat for Humanity International
121 Habitat Street
Americus, GA 31709
Telephone: 229-924-6935, ext. 2551 or 2552
E-mail: publicinfo@hfhi.org
http://www.habitat.org

In recent years, Habitat for Humanity has become one of the most prominent forces in reducing poverty, homelessness and inadequate housing in America and abroad. Its volunteers work to build and repair quality houses for families at no charge (residents pay a no-interest mortgage). Volunteer opportunities go beyond construction work. There is promotion, recruitment and countless other activities available. This is a Christian-based organization, and can be found in cities across the country.

HERO Homeless Empowerment Relationship Organization
2302 Lapeer Road
Suite H
Flint, MI 48503
Telephone: 810-239-3089

HERO offers crisis management services as well as programs designed to end homelessness by addressing its root causes. HERO forms one-on-one partnerships between homeless individuals, known as Partners, and mentoring volunteers. HERO is developing a national network of Campus Affiliates and community-based partnership programs. To accomplish this, HERO is seeking individuals who can take the lead in their communities. If you would like more information, contact HERO.

Jewish Community Centers Association of North America
15 East 26th Street
New York, NY 10010-1579
Telephone: 212-532-4958
Website: http://www.jcca.org

Jewish Community Centers are found in towns and cities all over the country, each addressing the unique needs of that area. The most common services required and offered are those for children, the elderly, homeless individuals and families. The association is also very active in improving intercultural relations.

Mothers Against Drunk Driving
511 East John Carpenter Freeway, Suite 700
Irving, TX 75062
Telephone: 972-869-2206 / 800-GET-MADD (438-6233)
Website: http://www.madd.org

The mission behind MADD: to establish the public conviction that drunk driving is unacceptable and criminal. It works with victims, their families and allies to influence public policies, programs and legislation. MADD has over half a million members in nearly 400 chapters across the country.

National 4-H Council
7100 Connecticut Avenue
Chevy Chase, MD 20815
Telephone: 301-961-2800
http://www.fourhcouncil.edu

The 4-H program is operated under the Extension Service of the U.S. Department of Agriculture and the State Land Grant University System. Through the Council, more than half-a-million volunteers work with boys and girls to boost their self-esteem and to teach the value of both community service and our natural resources. Programs run by 4-H also empower young people to become self-directed and productive in society.

National Association on Volunteers in Criminal Justice
University of Wisconsin-Milwaukee
Criminal Justice Institute
P.O. Box 786
Milwaukee, WI 53201
Telephone: 414-229-5630

Volunteers through the NAVCJ are committed to improving the

juvenile and criminal justice system through participation and education. The organization has more than 300,000 volunteers across the country.

National Black Child Development Institute
1463 Rhode Island Avenue, NW
Washington, DC 20005
Telephone: 202-673-7700
Website: http://www.nbcdi.org

This non-profit organization aims to serve African-American youth across the country. Through its affiliate network, it provides services in health, child welfare, education and child care. It also serves an advocacy function by monitoring government policies and laws that affect African-American children.

National Center for Youth Law
405 Fourteenth Street
15th Floor
Oakland, CA 94612-2701
Telephone: 510-835-8098
Website: http://www.youthlaw.org

Those students pursuing law careers may be interested in opportunities with this organization which focuses solely on helping attorneys and legal assistants who represent and defend the rights of poor children. The organization works on a nationwide basis. It supports legal consultation and training and publishes relevant information.

National Student Campaign Against Hunger and Homelessness
233 North Pleasant Avenue
Amherst, MA 01002
Telephone: 413-253-6417 / 800-NO HUNGR (664-8647)
E-mail: nscah@aol.com
Website: http://www.nscahh.org

If hunger and homelessness is a major concern to you, then you may be interested in joining this national coalition of students who work to solve these problems. Volunteers play a big part in delivering meals to the hungry from restaurants and dining halls. But they are also involved in public education and advocacy regarding the root causes of these problems in our society, through a variety of services and projects. Call them to find out if there is a coalition near you. If not, maybe you can start one!

The National Urban League, Inc.
120 Wall Street
New York, NY 10005
Telephone: 212-558-5300
E-mail: info@nul.org
http://www.nul.org

The National Urban League, through its 113 affiliates and 30,000 volunteers, aims to secure equal opportunities for all Americans, regardless of their racial or ethnic background. Services include assistance in job placement and training, housing, health care and research in social and economic concerns. It plays a vital role in advocacy and in public awareness of issues dealing with equality.

Neighborhood Reinvestment Corporation
NeighborWorks
1325 G Street, NW, Suite 800
Washington, DC 20005
Telephone: 202-220-2300
Website: http://www.nw.org

The broken neighborhoods in our cities were not built that way. The focus of Neighborhood Reinvestment Corporation (NRC) and NeighborWorks is to encourage investment in those neighborhoods, through partnerships between volunteers, paid staff and residents. Services include processing loans, fund raising and media coverage. Like Habitat for Humanity, this program has helped renovate over a hundred thousand homes across the country and is active in 139 cities.

Project Head Start
National Head Start Association
1651 Prince Street
Alexandria, VA 22314
Telephone: 703-739-0875
Website: http://www.nhsa.org

Project Head Start is a federally funded program to help under-privileged children ages three to five build self-confidence and gain the nutritional, educational and family support they will need to live productive lives. Through schools, churches and community centers across the nation, volunteers and staff help provide children (including the disabled) in those basic areas. Many other non-profit organizations are involved with Head Start.

The Salvation Army
615 Slaters Lane
P.O. Box 269
Alexandria, VA 22313
E-mail: Information@usn.salvationarmy.org
Website: http://www.salvationarmyusa.org

A Church in itself, "Salvationists" endeavor to do the work of the Lord through action and spreading the Gospel of Jesus Christ. The Army operates shelters and soup kitchens around the country, and provides a multitude of services to individuals, children and families, including adult rehabilitation for nonviolent offenders and treatment for those dealing with substance abuse. At Christmas, the Army distributes toys and gifts to children, and is famous for their annual yuletide collection kettles. Contact your local Salvation Army to see how they might need you.

America's Second Harvest
35 East Wacker Drive #2000
Chicago, IL 60601
Telephone: 312-263-2303 / 800-771-2303
Website: http://www.secondharvest.org

If you have ever seen or been to a local food bank, where hungry Americans are able to collect dry and canned groceries to feed their families, chances are that food bank has been supported in part by Second Harvest. Since 1979, Second Harvest has assisted in getting nearly four billion pounds of food shipped across the country to food banks, pantries, shelters and other charitable agencies.

United Neighborhood Centers of America, Inc.
3631 Perkins Avenue
4th Floor
Cleveland, OH 44114-4705
Phone: 216-391-3028
E-mail: unca@en.com
Website: http://www.unca.org

This national, non-profit voluntary organization has affiliates all over the country which respond to specific community needs. These include the most prevalent: youth violence, homelessness and other problems related to poverty. Substance abuse and illiteracy are also addressed through their neighborhood centers. There are a wide variety of volunteer opportunities.

Volunteers of America
1660 Duke Street
Alexandria, VA 22314
Telephone: 703-341-5000 / 800-899-0089
E-mail: voa@voa.org
Website: http://www.voa.org

Volunteers of America is a Christian-based human services organization found in 300 cities around the country. They provide meals for elderly people and offer day care services for families. They receive second-hand clothing and other items for their resale stores and provide other services needed in their communities.

Young Men's Christian Association
101 North Wacker Drive
Chicago, IL 60606
Telephone: 312-977-0031
Website: http://www.ymca.net

A worldwide movement that began in England over a century ago, the YMCA has consistently dedicated itself to serving the whole person: mind, body and spirit. In recent decades, the YMCA has done much to serve the needs of children and families, and is the nation's largest provider of childcare. Call your local YMCA to find out about the limitless service opportunities.

Young Women's Christian Association
Empire State Building
350 Fifth Avenue
Suite 301
New York, NY 10118
Telephone: 212-273-7800
Website: http://www.ywca.org

Each year, nearly two million women, girls and their families benefit from YWCA services around the country. The YWCA has dedicated itself to addressing the specific problems that threaten families, women and children. These include domestic violence, drug abuse, homelessness and racism. The YWCA is also a strong advocate for women's issues on both the local and national levels.

Educational Organizations

Campus Compact
Box 1975
Brown University
Providence, RI 02912
Telephone: 401-867-3950
Website: http://www.compact.org

Founded in 1985 by small group of college presidents, Campus Compact is a coalition of higher education leaders committed to Service Learning, which integrates service into the academic curriculum. The organization works successfully on the local and national levels to apply community service to all fields, and works with faculty to do so successfully. (For more information on Service Learning and Campus Compact, see chapter 9.)

Christian Literacy Associates
Allegheny County Literacy Council
541 Perry Highway
Pittsburgh, PA 15229
Telephone: 412-364-3777

Through CLA, thousands of volunteers all over the country teach reading with the Bible. Tutoring is done on an individual basis, and students also learn about the key points of Christianity while they learn to read. If you are interested in Bible study and literacy, then give them a call. If no local program exists, then you might be able to start one.

Communities in Schools, Inc.
1199 North Fairfax Street #300
Alexandria, VA 22314
Telephone: 703-519-8999 / 800-CIS-KIDS (247-5437)
Website: http://www.cisnet.org

Communities in Schools is a national organization dedicated to preventing at-risk youth from dropping out of school. They operate more than 200 sites across the nation, and form support groups of volunteers in health, education and other backgrounds to help kids develop positive attitudes about their education and work. Volunteers provide services such as tutoring, skills training and positive recreational activities.

Contact Center Inc.
P.O. Box 81826
Lincoln, NE 68501
Telephone: 402-464-0602 / 800-228-8813

This is one of the most comprehensive programs geared to ending illiteracy in America. If you are interested in stopping illiteracy, but don't know where to begin, then Contact Center can serve as a networking tool to put you in touch with someone you can help. As part of its mission, it also has a collection of publications that help volunteer tutors in many ways, and publishes a newsletter focusing on ending illiteracy.

I Have a Dream Foundation
330 Seventh Avenue
20th Floor
New York, NY 10001
Telephone: 212-293-5480
Website: http://www.ihad.org

This organization works through individuals and local organizations, funding I Have a Dream projects, which all strive to empower sponsored students to achieve their educational and employment goals. It conducts seminars and training programs to enable individuals to build their own futures.

Learning Disabilities Association of America
4156 Library Road
Pittsburgh, PA 15234
Telephone: 412-341-1515
Website: http://www.ldanatl.org

This organization focuses on a broad spectrum of learning disabilities including the forms, causes and consequences. It strives to increase public awareness, improve education and research, promote advocacy and create opportunities for those with such disabilities. It does this through chapters in all fifty states, and distributes many publications to promote awareness. Call the main office to find out more about the chapter nearest you.

National Association of Partners in Education
901 North Pitt Street
Suite 320
Alexandria, VA 22314
Telephone: 703-836-4880
E-mail: napehq@napehq.org
Website: http://www.napehq.org

More than four million parents, retired professionals, educators and active business people participate in this nationwide program aimed at strengthening the bonds between public education and the community. It involves tutoring students, and other special projects such as aiding a school's physical or management needs, or teaching special programs for students related to sexual issues, career guidance or drug education.

National PTA

330 North Wabash Street
Suite 2100
Chicago, IL 60611
Telephone: 312-670-6782 / 800-307-4782
Website: http://www.pta.org

The National Parent Teachers Association involves more than just teachers. It is for anyone with an interest in the future of our nation's children. Nationwide, it boasts more than six million members in its more than 25,000 local chapters. Programs include substance abuse prevention, increasing cultural awareness, promoting safety and enhancing the educational experience.

ProLiteracy Worldwide

1320 Jamesville Avenue
Syracuse, NY 13210
Telephone: 800-528-2224
Website: http://www.laubach.org *or*
http://www.literacyvolunteers.org

ProLiteracy Worldwide was recently established through the merging of the two largest adult volunteer literacy organizations in the world: Laubach Literacy International and Literacy Volunteers of America (LVA). It is comprised of independent, volunteer-based adult literacy programs across the country and around the world. Nearly 350,000 people each year receive services in English instruction as a second language as well as in basic literacy. If you would like a volunteer opportunity that provides a wealth of support and training, you may want to check them out. They may even support you in starting a program in your own community.

Reading is Fundamental
1825 Connecticut Avenue, NW
Suite 400
Washington, DC 20009
Telephone: 202-673-0020 / 800-RIF-READ (743-7323)
Website: http://www.rif.org

RIF uses its nearly 100,000 volunteers across the country to organize and conduct imaginative activities for children, generating a greater interest in reading. It is essentially a grass-roots organization, with RIF centers in nearly every city.

Student Pugwash USA
2029 P Street, NW
Suite 301
Washington, DC 20036
Telephone: 202-429-8900
E-mail: spusa@spusa.org
Website: http://www.spusa.org

College and high school students can learn about careers in technology and science, and how those pursuits affect our society. This organization provides students with information on these issues and their related career opportunities. Its chapters across the country are run by students and young professionals, and offer many publications. For more information, call the number above.

Health and Disabilities Groups

Alzheimer's Association
70 North Michigan Avenue
Suite 1100
Chicago, IL 60611-1676
Telephone: 312-335-8700 / 800-272-3900
E-mail: info@alz.org
Website: http://www.alz.org

ADRDA serves all victims of Alzheimer's and related disorders. This includes both patients and their families. The organization supports research, education and advocacy, and provides support to family members. With close to 200 chapters across the country, volunteers are a primary force in carrying out this mission.

American Foundation for the Blind

11 Penn Plaza
Suite 300
New York, NY 10001
Telephone: 212-502-7600 / 800-232-5463
E-mail: afbinfo@afb.net
Website: http://www.afb.org

The American Foundation for the Blind works through over 700 schools and organizations across the nation, to serve the needs of visually impaired individuals. It does this in many ways, including direct support, education publications, consultation and advocacy. The organization has a wide variety of volunteer opportunities.

American Cancer Society

1599 Clifton Road
Atlanta, GA 30329
Telephone: 800-ACS-2345 (227-2345)
Website: http://www.cancer.org

The American Cancer Society is dedicated to eliminating cancer through prevention, research for cures and building awareness. Volunteers serve at all levels of the organization. You can easily find your local office by checking in your phone book or calling the number above.

American Diabetes Association

1701 North Beauregard Street
Alexandria, VA 22311
Telephone: 703-549-1500 / 800-342-2383
Website: http://www.diabetes.org

Through nearly 900 chapters and affiliates, staff and volunteers focus on research, service and fund-raising for those with diabetes and their families. They also build awareness and support research for cures and preventive treatment of diabetes.

American Foundation for AIDS Research
120 Wall Street
13th Floor
New York, NY 10005-3902
Telephone: 212-806-1600 / 800-39-amfar (392-3227)
Website: http://www.amfar.org

AmFAR is the nation's largest private sector funding organization dedicated solely to AIDS research, education and public policy. Volunteer opportunities exist across the country and include fund-raising events, research activities and administrative work.

American Heart Association
7320 Greenville Avenue
Dallas, TX 75231
Telephone: 214-373-6300 / 800-242-8721
Website: http://www.americanheart.org

With branches in communities across the nation and around the world, the American Heart Association boasts a vast network of volunteers totaling more than two million. Its primary function is to support research, prevention and education regarding stroke, heart disease and other cardiovascular problems. If you are interested, visit their website and fill out the volunteer form on-line for opportunities to serve either locally or nationally.

American Lung Association
61 Broadway
6th Floor
New York, NY 10006
Telephone: 212-315-8700
Website:http://www.lungusa.org

The American Lung Association is dedicated to the control and prevention of all lung diseases. They sponsor many educational awareness campaigns on the dangers of smoking, air pollution and occupational lung hazards. Volunteers are key to conducting activities and raising money, which goes to education and research. Like the American Heart Association website, the American Lung Association website also has an on-line volunteer form to fill out if you wish to assist the organization.

The ARC (formerly the Association for Retarded Citizens)
1010 Wayne Avenue
Suite 650
Silver Spring, MD 20910
Telephone: 301-565-3842
E-mail: info@thearc.org
Website: http://www.thearc.org

The ARC advocates the belief that all children and adults with mental retardation and related developmental disabilities have individual worth and potential. Through a strong volunteer base in 1,300 state and local chapters, volunteers assist members and their families through advocacy, obtaining support services and care, building community awareness, serving on committees and developing educational programs.

National Easter Seal Society
230 West Monroe Street
Suite 1800
Chicago, IL 60606
Telephone: 312-726-6200 / 800-221-6827
Website: http://www.easter-seals.org

The National Easter Seal Society is dedicated to increasing independence for those with disabilities. Through local branches, the society sponsors programs that offer physical and occupational therapy, communication and vocational guidance. Recreational and counseling services may also be offered, depending on local needs. Volunteers are needed at all levels, including board leadership, one-on-one service and fund raising.

National Mental Health Association
201 North Beauregard Street
12th Floor
Alexandria, VA 22311
Telephone: 703-684-7722 / 800-969-6642
Website: http://www.nmha.org
 The National Mental Health Association (NMHA) is a volunteer-based advocacy organization that deals with all aspects of mental illness, including its effect upon families. NMHA has worked to educate the public on the realities and effects of mental illness, and also to eliminate the discrimination which often occurs. Volunteers are actively recruited and trained to help those suffering from mental illness and their families. The National Mental Health Association is a large and well-established organization, with a variety of volunteer opportunities.

National Multiple Sclerosis Society
733 Third Avenue
New York, NY 10017
Telephone: 212-986-3240 / 800-344-4867
Website: http://www.nmss.org
 The National Multiple Sclerosis Society supports worldwide research on the cause, prevention, treatment and cure of MS. It operates close to 150 chapters nationwide and provides a variety of services, including counseling for victims and their families, self-help groups, physical fitness programs, medical services, rehabilitation services and advocacy.

Recording for the Blind and Dyslexic
20 Roszel Road
Princeton, NJ 08540
Telephone: 609-452-0606
Volunteer information: 800-803-7201
Website: http://www.rfbd.org
 Recording for the Blind began as a small volunteer organization that now operates nationwide. Volunteers are needed to read books

and other resources aloud for recording. There is a special need for volunteers with science and math backgrounds. If you can speak clearly, or would like to refine your speaking skills, then it may be worth a phone call.

United Cerebral Palsy National
1660 L Street, NW
Suite 700
Washington, DC 20036
Telephone: 202-776-0406 / 800-872-5827
Website: http://www.ucpa.org

As one of the largest health charities in America, United Cerebral Palsy National's mission is to advance the independence, productivity and full citizenship of people with cerebral palsy and other disabilities. Volunteers work busily in communities to help children and adults with cerebral palsy as well as their families. These services include special education, social and recreational activities, as well as local advocacy.

Cultural Organizations

American Association of Museums (or your local museum)
1225 Eye Street, NW
Suite 400
Washington, DC 20005
Telephone: 202-289-1818
Website: http://www.aam-us.org

The Association works diligently on the national level to advance the support and success of our nation's museums. Many of our nation's museums would simply not exist if not for the support of volunteers at all levels. Volunteering in this area can present a tremendous opportunity to increase personal interaction with others and improve communication skills. You may even learn a thing or two about art, science or history. Contact your local museum or AAM affiliate (often on the state level) for more information.

National Public Radio
635 Massachusetts Avenue, NW
Washington, DC 20001
Telephone: 202-513-2000
Website: http://www.npr.org

You may have already read about the benefits of being an NPR listener, but have you thought about volunteering at your local NPR station? The most obvious opportunity is answering phones during their pledge drives. But others exist as well, including assistance with local programming. Give them a call and check it out.

Environmental and Animal Protection Organizations

American Society for the Prevention of Cruelty to Animals (ASPCA)
424 East 92nd Street
New York, NY 10128
Telephone: 212-876-7700

The ASPCA exists to promote humane principles, prevent cruelty and alleviate fear, pain and suffering in the lives of animals. Among their many services and initiatives are public service announcements about animal cruelty, urging people to adopt animals from shelters, lobbying for animal protection and providing medical care and shelter to abused, neglect and abandoned animals and pet adoption services. Although the ASPCA is located in New York City, there are similar non-profit organizations (SPCAs) located around the country in every state that need the help of volunteers. Just search for "SPCA" on the Internet to find one in your area or visit your local animal shelter.

Animal Rights Mobilization!
P.O. Box 1553
Williamsport, PA 17703
Telephone: 717-322-3252

This is a grass-roots network of groups across the country, dedicated to eradicating animal abuse and exploitation. ARM! is involved in highly visible, dramatic events to further its cause. If you feel that this may be a worth a look, then contact your local group, or call their national headquarters.

Clean Water Action
4455 Connecticut Avenue, NW
Suite A300
Washington, DC 20008-2328
Telephone: 202-895-0420
Website: http://www.cleanwateraction.org

Clean Water Action is the only organization solely dedicated to protecting our waters along the Atlantic shore, the Great Lakes, the Gulf and the New England coast. It has sponsored campaigns against pollution with toxic chemicals, and has successfully lobbied water-friendly legislation. They have twenty-four offices nationwide, and can use volunteer support in a variety of activities.

Earthwatch
3 Clock Tower Place
Suite 100
Box 75
Maynard, MA 01754
Telephone: 978-461-0081 / 800-776-0188
E-mail: info@earthwatch.org
Website: http://www.earthwatch.org

More than 15,000 volunteers support Earthwatch in its efforts to preserve the world's endangered habitats and species. With the support of underwriters, Earthwatch actively conducts research expeditions and educates the public on matters of science and nature. It is an international movement, and offers a multitude of experiential opportunities in the form of volunteerism and internships for young people.

The Humane Society of the United States
2100 L Street, NW
Washington, DC 20037
Telephone: 202-452-1100
Website: http:www.hsus.org

The Humane Society of the United States aims to make a difference in the lives of animals at home and worldwide. The HSUS is dedicated to creating a world where our relationship with animals is guided by compassion. Their services and initiatives include legislative lobbying, providing information to pet owners and educational programs through universities, fighting for wildlife habitat protection and marine mammal protection and offering community programs through HSUS's ten regional offices.

The Izaak Walton League of America
707 Conservation Lane
Gaithersburg, MD 20878
Telephone: 301-548-0150 / 800-453-5463
E-mail: general@iwla.org
Website: http://www.iwla.org

This is a conservation organization that is dedicated to protecting our planet's natural resources. Most of the members are outdoorsmen and women who are affiliated through the more than 400 chapters across the country. The League may be an appealing opportunity if you are interested in getting involved in grass-roots conservation efforts. The League also sponsors educational programs for children and adults, instructs on hunting safety and is involved in advocacy.

Kids Against Pollution
P.O. Box 775
Closter, NJ 07624
Telephone: 201-784-0668

What began as a group of elementary school children trying to raise awareness of the dangers of toxic pollution in New Jersey has now grown to a non-profit nationwide organization of over a thousand chapters. If you would like to become involved in both child education and environmental protection, then this may be the place to look.

National Audubon Society
700 Broadway
New York, NY 10003
Telephone: 212-929-3000
Website: http://www.audubon.org

The National Audubon Society has over half a million members in more than 500 local chapters across the United States. Their members work at all levels to preserve our natural resources and heritage. It also protects a nationwide reserve of 250,000 acres for wildlife. Service opportunities include participation in conservation efforts, education and influencing legislation.

The Nature Conservancy
4245 North Fairfax Drive
Suite 100
Arlington, VA 22203-1606
Telephone: 703-841-5300
E-mail: comment@tnc.org
Website: http://nature.org

The mission of The Nature Conservancy (TNC) is to preserve the plants, animals and natural communities that represent the diversity of life on Earth by protecting the lands and waters they need to survive. Since 1951, TNC has worked with communities, businesses and individuals to protect more than 98 million acres around the world. TNC is looking for volunteers who love working outdoors, sharing their love of nature with others and believe in land conservation. They need help in a variety of areas including maintenance and management of trails, parks, open fields, beaches and other natural habitats, public relations by assisting in education at informational nature centers and public speaking at various venues and office administrative work.

Pesticide Action Network North America
49 Powell Street
Suite 500
San Francisco, CA 94102
Telephone: 415-981-1771
E-mail: panna@panna.org
Website: http://www.panna.org

This is a non-profit organization that is part of the much larger
PAN International. It is made up of 300 independent citizen organizations working to achieve pesticide reform all over the world. It is heavily involved in education and produces numerous publications to promote awareness. If you are studying agriculture, chemistry or any
other of the sciences, you may want to check this group out.

Appendix II

Campus and Community Resources

Throughout this book, I have repeatedly referred to all the different resources and organizations available to you in your community and on campus. You have read about using your school's career or academic offices. You know by now that there are a host of clubs and professional organizations in your area. Here, I would like to refer you to a few other resources that have not been previously mentioned.

Fraternities and Sororities

Also referred to as Greek Letter Societies, these are organizations made up of college students and alumni which have pledge membership to one another. There are four basic types:

General or Social Greek organizations draw students from a wide range of backgrounds. These organizations make up the majority of all memberships in the nation.

Professional fraternities or sororities are organizations which attract members with a similar course of study or career plans. They often will also require a minimum GPA, and usually have tougher admission standards. However, their activities and programs, not to mention contacts through alumni, can be very helpful to you in jump-starting your career.

Honor Societies are groups which generally choose their members for their high academic achievements.

Recognition Societies are groups which choose members who are recognized for great achievements in specific areas or professions.

Most Greek letter organizations have chapters at colleges and universities around the country. While they are often known for social activities, they can also provide tremendous opportunities for you to jump-start your career. Many of them sponsor charitable activities and some do career fairs and other related events.

Professional fraternities and sororities can be very useful. If there is one on your campus that is geared towards your chosen field, you may want to check it out. Membership will provide access to educational resources, work and internship opportunities and alumni who are established in their professions.

Development Councils
It's in their interest to help you!

Most cities and communities have some form of development council, which might act similarly to a chamber of commerce. These councils are geared toward encouraging and nurturing economic development in the area. This is accomplished by:

- attracting outside companies to locate in the area, thus increasing local employment opportunities
- representing and advocating the best interests of existing businesses
- developing partnerships with other community organizations such as professional associations, the Small Business Administration and other major employers
- serving the interests and needs of individuals searching for work or seeking to relocate to the region

These are broad-based activities, and I will be the first to tell you that no two chambers of commerce are alike. It depends on the nature of the community and the leadership. In some smaller towns, the development office is not even open 40 hours a week, while in very large cities, the office might be a lot more ambitious. Regardless of where you find them, the councils will have a customer service attitude, and are more than willing to help.

How to make use of your Development Council:

- Get one of their directories, and use it to become familiar with area businesses. Most of your well established businesses will be members. Often, these guides are divided up by industry, and will also indicate how many employees the businesses have.
- Attend their events and gatherings. While many chambers sponsor "networking" parties, they also have speakers, sponsor luncheons and a host of other activities tied to business development. Some even have special interest groups of individuals and companies with related interests or in related industries.
- Volunteer or get a job in your local chamber office. What better way to become familiar and perhaps connected with key business people in the community?

The regional chamber of commerce or development council can be a valuable resource. It is in the office's best interest to help you, because it is in the community's best interest for you to get connected, be productive and contribute to the area's overall quality of life.

Appendix III

Media Resources

What follows are print and Internet resources that may be a valuable asset to you as you jump-start your career. Most of them can be obtained through your local bookstore and are available at your library. All titles included here are recommended reading.

CAREER WEBSITES FOR COLLEGE STUDENTS
About Internet Resources

For the sake of brevity (and the focus of this book, which is *not* about job-hunting), I have included a list here of among the best and most popular career sites on the net, geared specifically towards college students. As you are likely aware, many more exist, as well as those for more experienced job seekers.

Most of these sites have the following in common:

1. they list job openings
2. provide a wealth of excellent "how-to" information
3. provide resources on various companies
4. allow you to post your resume

Let's face it: the Internet is a great medium. It makes accessing information a snap—far easier than it used to be. But, it is still *just a tool* at your disposal. You may research companies, you may find openings, you can uncover potential opportunities, but don't let this convenience fool you. Two *computers* shaking hands is no substitute for two *people* shaking hands. You still must take the step to make *personal* contact. You need to build relationships. That will never change.

An additional word about "posting" your resume...

As indicated, virtually every career site out there allows you to post your resume—allowing others to view it without you knowing it. Is this a good thing? Others may disagree, but my sense is that it's not. Here's what you may expect if you choose to post your resume on multiple online boards and sites:

- a lot of work for you (keying in the information, keeping track of multiple usernames and passwords for each site, etc.).
- the frustration of keeping all your resumes consistent and updated (you won't).
- very few (if any at all) calls from potential employers or recruiters wishing to discuss legitimate opportunities.
- occasional calls from people looking to get you in on a network marketing scheme. Primerica has become notorious for that.

Suffice it to say, I do not believe that posting your resume is necessarily worth all the hassle. Employers will use these services to post openings, but they will seldom search through the zillions of resumes that are already there (Okay, I admit it...mine's one of them!).

Peterson's Education and Career Center
http://www.petersons.com

This is a great Web site for people of virtually all ages. It includes information and keys to many levels of learning, from grade school to graduate school. It has information and resources on applying to college, finding internships and looking for work.

Kaplan Career Center

http://www.kaplan.com/career

Designed primarily for college students, this Web site, as well as the sponsoring organization, provides information on career selection, the hidden job market, writing resumes and letters, interviewing entrepreneurship. It also has information on testing and classes offered around the country.

JobWeb

http://www.jobweb.org

This site is sponsored by the National Association of Colleges and Employers. Its objective is to bridge the gap between higher education and the world of work. Through this site, you can review articles, get tips and view job listings.

Monster.com

http://www.monster.com

Monster.com is one if the biggest and best-known career resources on the web. It features all that you would find on the other job-hunting sites, but also has a special area for college students.

College Grad Job Hunter

http://www.collegegrad.com

College Grad targets the needs of college students and recent grads exclusively, with entry-level job search content for job seekers. A well-organized and long standing resource (they've been around since 1995—an eternity in computer years!).

College Recruiter

http://www.collegerecruiter.com

College Recruiter is the highest traffic, non-password protected site used by job hunting students and recent graduates and the employers who want to hire them. They help employers hire college students, grads and recent graduates. Employers pay to post job openings and for access to a resume bank. They also have an "ask the experts" feature where a visitor presents a question or dilemma and you get to see how a fairly diverse group of experts respond, all at the same time (I am one of them.)

Experience
http://www.experience.com

Experience is both a magazine and a website. You can receive a subscription for free. It provides useful information and allows you to learn from the experiences of others. They also have a strong partnership with campus career centers around the country.

CampusCareerCenter.com
http://www.campuscareercenter.com

Campus Career Center offers connectivity between students, college career centers and companies across the country. An ambitious grass roots student representative program is one of the organization's distinctive features.

CollegeJournal.com
http://www.collegejournal.com

CollegeJournal is the premier free site for undergraduate, graduate and MBA students who want job-search and career-guidance information. Content comes from the Wall Street Journal, as well as from the CollegeJournal.com editorial team. Content is updated daily and includes news, features and trends helpful for college students and entry-level candidates.

CollegeCentral.com
http://www.collegecentral.com

Well designed, College Central is a "network" of four entities: Student Central, Alumni Central, Employer Central and Career Services Central. You can obviously guess the audience for each entity—and the site draws a wealth of helpful information.

Jobpostings.net
http://www.jobpostings.net

A site geared for students, JobPostings.net offers articles and resources, as well as company profiles and information on areas like government and health care. It also follows the format of an electronic magazine.

College Job Board
http://www.collegejobboard.com

College Job Board claims to be "a job board for everyone: students and alumni of every college, university, graduate school, high school, and vocational and adult education school in the United States." CollegeJobBoard is designed to help students and alumni find internships, temporary jobs, part-time jobs and full-time jobs. Employers can also post job openings to individual schools.

AfterCollege™
http://www.aftercollege.com

AfterCollege™ is a service for college students and recent graduates who are looking for jobs, internships and other opportunities. It's been around for a while—started in October 1996 by two students at Stanford University. Five months later, it obtained national recognition by being featured as a USA Today Hot Site.

Careerfair.com
http://www.careerfair.com

This site is designed for the college and professional job seeker. It offers both on-line and physical career fairs that help get your resume (and your face) in front of America's top employers.

AboutJobs.com
http://www.aboutjobs.com

This site positions itself as a resource for "students, recent graduates, expatriates and adventure-seekers." It's a gateway to four different categories: SummerJobs, OverseasJobs, InternJobs and ResortJobs.

VOLUNTEER SERVICE AND COMMUNITY SERVICE

Listed here are books and publications that provide valuable advice and information on getting in involved in volunteer and community service.

Students in Service to America: A Guidebook for Engaging America's Students in a Lifelong Habit of Service
by USA Freedom Corps
(Available free in PDF format at www.usafreedomcorps.org.)

Following the events of September 11, 2001, President George W. Bush called on all Americans to commit at least 4,000 hours—the equivalent of two years—over the course of their lives to the service of others. By contributing your time and effort to a cause greater than yourself, you learn about the rich democratic traditions of America, help meet vital community needs and become a responsible and engaged citizen.

Beyond Success: How Volunteer Service can Help You Begin Making a Life Instead of Just a Living
by John F. Raynolds III and Eleanor Raynolds, CBE

This is a great book which, at times, seems to be speaking directly to professionals who have achieved a certain level of success, and are now asking, "Is this all there is?"

The answer is, of course not! Throughout this book, the authors illustrate—with many examples and stories—how each of us has the capacity to positively influence our world. It emphasizes how a community-service approach can re-energize our careers and refresh us from the often-encountered job doldrums.

It includes information on the many ways each of us can serve the needs of our communities, and offers specific advice on how to keep our volunteer service from falling the way of many boring or lackluster jobs. It also provides information on many types of non-profit organizations.

Volunteer USA
by Andrew Carroll

This is regarded as a classic volume in the area of volunteer service, with tons of information on resources, causes and organizations for the individual looking for a niche in community service.

Volunteer USA has an extremely comprehensive guide to both regional and national non-profit organizations. If you want a deeper level of advice on the dos and don'ts of community service, and how to benefit the most from it, then read this book.

Service Learning: A Guide for College Students
by National Center for Service-Learning, ACTION
and
Combining Service and Learning: A Resource Book for Community and Public Service, Volume II
by National Society for Experiential Education

For deeper insight into service and internship opportunities you can create for yourself to advance your career and education, then these two books are worth a look. Both books can be extremely helpful in seeking out or creating a community service project that directly correlates to your chosen field.

Revolution of the Heart: A New Strategy for Creating Wealth and Meaningful Change
by Bill Shore

In a relatively short book, Bill Shore, founder of *Share Our Strength*, points out how we must re-examine the very definition of citizenship if we are to improve our future. He questions our priorities as a society which rallies to the support of a little girl trapped in a well, while millions of starving and neglected children go unnoticed each day.

He also reinforces the holistic approach to careers pointed out here: the importance of seeking employment, volunteer service or a business in terms of how one uses them to improve other peoples' lives.

Welcome to the Real World: You've Got an Education, Now Get a Life!
by Stacy Kravetz

While this book is aimed at college *graduates*, I still recommend it to students. It's an introduction to the real world, or at least aspects of the world you may not have had to deal with yet. It covers a wide range of topics, from finding a job to getting your own apartment and car to managing your finances.

PERSONAL GROWTH AND RELATIONSHIPS

Unlimited Power
by Anthony Robbins

This book is highly intense reading. While the information is pretty complex, addressing topics from neurolinguistic programming to the overwhelming benefits of living on a vegan diet, its overall message is fairly simple—to succeed in this world, you must first be able to effectively *communicate with yourself.*

Robbins also makes some compelling historical references to emphasize the power which our minds have over our bodies.

A World Waiting to Be Born: Civility Rediscovered
by M. Scott Peck, M.D.

In Peck's own terms, this is a book largely about organizational behavior. It is a deep, spiritual and psychological analysis of how we as human beings treat and relate to one another.

Since we have already established the importance of relationships with others, this is highly recommended reading for any person interested in a deeper understanding of human relationships on all levels.

The Seven Habits of Highly Effective People: Restoring the Character Ethic
by Stephen R. Covey

No book has been recommended to me by others as often as this one. It puts some very important topics into a clearer perspective, which include: setting goals, looking at situations from another's point of view, developing listening skills and examining time management in terms of life management.

First Things First
by Stephen R. Covey, A. Roger Merrill, Rebecca R. Merrill

Effective time management is one of the "Seven Habits" which Covey introduced in his work listed above. Managing time is probably one of the toughest challenges you will face daily as you mature and your responsibilities increase.

First Things First makes you ask yourself, *Do I know where I am heading in life? Or am I just trying to survive the day?*

Lead the Field (audio program)
by Earl Nightingale

What I love most about *Lead the Field* is its profound simplicity in explaining the values and principles which guide us.

Nightingale describes these common-sense principles, many of which have been around for quite a while. But the key messages are very clear: Do what you enjoy. Do it for the benefit of others. The more you give with a positive attitude, the more you get back. It gets more inspirational with each repeated listening.

INTERNSHIPS AND SUMMER EMPLOYMENT

Peterson's Internships
by Peterson's Education Center (www.petersons.com)

This book is a fantastic resource for students seeking internship opportunities in a wide variety of fields. Thousands of companies, non-profit organizations and government agencies are listed with over 40,000 opportunities available. Each listing indicates the number of opportunities available in various positions, the pay status and specific application instructions. Among the best features are the indexes, which cross-reference all opportunities by specific field of interest, geographic area and name of employer. This guide is updated annually.

Internships: The Hotlist for Job Hunters
by Sara Dulaney Gilbert

This is another helpful guide which lists employers all over the country with opportunities in a variety of fields. General categories listed are the arts, business, communications, culture/education, the environment, government, health care, international opportunities, public affairs, science/research, social services and associations. There are also listings of sources for those with special disabilities. This is also updated annually.

The Internship Bible
by Mark Oldman and Samer Hamadeh

This is a huge book which not only includes a vast array of opportunities listed by category (more than 100,000 claimed), but is also filled with stories and profiles of established people who have worked at various internships.

Peterson's Summer Jobs for Students
by Peterson's Education Center

This resource lists organizations by state which seek people primarily during the summer months. It also includes tips on applying for such jobs, as well as indexes by category, employer and job title.

Overseas Summer Jobs
by Peterson's Education Center

For those who want to work overseas, this resource indexes such opportunities available in more than fifty countries. It also includes very helpful information and advice on landing such jobs, and on how to get around bureaucratic obstacles.

SMALL BUSINESS

The Young Entrepreneur's Guide to Starting and Running a Business
by Steve Mariotti

So vitally important to any new business start-up is planning. Failure to plan is a key factor as to why so many businesses fail within their first year. Steve Mariotti, founder and president of the *National Foundation for Teaching Entrepreneurship*, emphasizes planning throughout this book and takes the reader step-by-step through the process. This guide to small business covers such topics as preparing a business plan, managing finances, doing research and advertising. It also helps you generate ideas to turn into successful enterprises, and provides stories of entrepreneurial successes.

555 Ways to Earn Extra Money
by Jay Conrad Levinson

This book, which is by the same author of the best-selling *Guerrilla Marketing*, is filled with creative ideas for small business enterprises. It discusses enterprises which can be maintained purely to supplement another income, or nurtured into full-time businesses on their own.

Starting on a Shoestring: Building a Business Without a Bankroll
by Arnold S. Goldstein, Ph.D.

This is a well-regarded book that is excellent reading if you are considering starting your own enterprise. You will get solid business advice, much of which you may not get in the lecture hall.

Relationship Selling: The Key to Getting and Keeping Customers
by Jim Cathcart, CPAE

Just as relationships are key to building a career, they are key to building a successful business and customer base. An insightful book, it helps you to see customers as people to be *served*, not people to be used.

The Power to Get In
by Michael A. Boylan

This is an incredible book that shows you how to get your foot into the door of places you never dreamed possible. The author has refined a system he calls the "Circle of Leverage," whereby you make your initial contact with not one, but several individuals in an organization at the same time. A must-read for job hunters or sales people.

JOB HUNTING

Resumes Don't Get Jobs: The Realities and Myths of Job Hunting
by Bob Weinstein

Of the many job-hunting books available, this is one of the few which is really in tune with the current job market. Weinstein dispels the conventional job-hunting myths, and urges the reader to be more creative and aggressive. It also shows you how to package yourself in an ever-shrinking job market. It's a little older and doesn't get into the technology of today, yet it is still an excellent resource.

"I'll Work for Free"—A Short-Term Strategy for a Long-Term Payoff
by Bob Weinstein

Weinstein, who specializes in innovative techniques to advance one's career, provides excellent advice that is particularly helpful for college students, although the book is targeted towards a greater audience. Indeed, offering your services for free (temporarily, of course) is an offer which can increase experience, lead to new contacts and open doors to more fulfilling opportunities.

How to Get Your Dream Job Using the Internet
by Shannon Bounds and Arthur Karl

A fantastic book, especially if you are not familiar with Internet terms. It provides an introduction on how technology is changing the way employers and job hunters find each other. It shows you how to track down companies on the Web, search their listings, and even post your resume and apply for a job via E-mail. A CD-ROM with some helpful programs is also provided.

Be Your Own Headhunter Online
by Pam Dixon and Sylvia Tiersten

This is another helpful resource in seeking job opportunities over the Internet which tells you how to use resources such as the World Wide Web, bulletin boards, free nets, commercial services and private employment databases.

Jobsmarts for Twentysomethings
by Bradley G. Richardson

This book focuses not only a job hunting, but on job survival. It is written by someone who is not too many years out of college himself. He addresses several key issues that the recent college grad will have to face when entering the job market.

OTHER TITLES OF INTEREST

The End of Work
by Jeremy Rifkin

If you are concerned about what the future holds for our economy, then this is a provocative and insightful book to read. Rifkin discusses the permanence of a shrinking labor force, the unending growth of technological advancements and the addition of foreign competition. The dilemma: what will our society do with a vast number of people for whom there are no jobs as we know them today?

Rifkin has been hailed for his insightfulness in predicting the biggest challenge of tomorrow's economy. Since we will be living in the future, we must do our best to anticipate its challenges. This is an excellent book to do just that.

Career Transitions in Turbulent Times: Exploring Work, Learning and Careers
Edited by Rich Feller and Garry Walz

This book offers compelling insights from more than fifty authors on the trends and innovations influencing career development. Primarily an academic work, it is published by ERIC Counseling & Student Services Clearinghouse.

OTHER RESOURCES

Encyclopedia of Associations

Want to find a group of people in your neighborhood with a particular interest or profession? This is the resource to use. It lists professional and social organizations, all of which are non-profit. There are also regional editions.

Journal of Career Planning and Employment
This is a periodical used mainly by career guidance counselors. It was very helpful in researching this book, and often has information that is extremely pertinent to the college student. I recommend going to your college library and looking through a couple of issues.

Appendix IV

Send Me Your Questions!

Since I wrote this book and have writing an ongoing newsletter feature of the same title, I have heard from many students and learned about some of their concerns. I would like to know more about you, how you felt this book was helpful and how it can be improved. This is all part of an ongoing research project aimed at these objectives: to help you understand and experience the reward of self-made challenges and to help you become successful at providing for yourself, your family and the community in which you live.

To help me accomplish these goals, I hope you will answer some of the following questions and send your responses to me by e-mail or through my website. Either way, to improve upon this book, I want to learn about your situation. I don't want you to just describe your successes; I want to hear about the obstacles and frustrations you have encountered as well.

Also, what questions do you have for me? Send them to me and I will try my best to answer them. You can reach me at:

E-mail: keithluscher@aol.com
Website: www.dontwaituntilyougraduate.com

In your message, please try to address the following:
- Educational institution you attend.
- Major or chosen field of study (if undecided, please say so).
- Expected year of graduation.
- What, if anything, are you doing right now to jump-start your career?
- What are your main concerns about obtaining a job after you graduate?
- What have been your biggest frustrations in preparing for your career?
- Have you had any successes or achievements of which you are proud? Please share!
- Are you active in community service, such as Service Learning programs, volunteerism or any other type of non-profit employment? If so, what kind of work is it and how is it helping you and those in your community?
- May I share your story with other readers (confidentially, of course)?

I hope you have learned a great deal after reading this book and I look forward to hearing from you!

Notes

Introduction

1. Earl Nightengale, *Lead the Field*, Audio program (Nightengale-Conant, Corp., 1986).
2. Paul Fidler and Constance Pritchard, "What Small Firms Look for in New Graduate Candidates," *Journal of Career Planning and Employment* (Spring 1993): 45.

Chapter 1

1. John Naisbitt and Patricia Aburdene. *Medatrends 2000* (New York: William Morrow and Co., 1999), 33.
2. "When Will the Layoffs End?" *Fortune*, 20 September 1993, 40.
3. Lawrence J. Bradford and Claire Raines, *Twentysomething: Managing and Motivating Today's New Work Force* (New York: MasterMedia Limited, 1991), 2.
4. Stephanie Armour, "Young Job Seekers Get Squeezed Out," *USA Today*, 15 August 2002.
5. Ibid.

Chapter 2

1. Tom Wolfe, *The Right Stuff* (New York: Farrar, Straus & Giroux, 1979), 53.

Chapter 3

1. Fidler and Pritchard, "What Small Firms Look for," 45.
2. Dr. Norman Vincent Peale, *Power of the Plus Factor* (Old Tappan, NY? NJ?: Fleming Revell, Co., 1987), 102.

Chapter 5

1. Harvey Mackay, *Sharkproof* (New York: HarperCollins, 1993), 66.

Chapter 6

1. Tony Carter, "Mentor Programs Belong in College, Too," *Journal of Career Planning and Employment*, Winter 1994, 51.
2. Kasandra Dalton McNeil, "Mentors Guide Students Through Challenges of College," *Chicago Tribune*, 20 July 1997, C25.
3. Eknath Easwaran, *Gandhi, the Man*, 2nd ed. (Petaluma, CA: Nilgin Press, 1978), 145.
4. David Leonhardt, "Class Acts in the Ivy-Colored Halls," *Business Week*, 16 December 1996, ENT19.

Chapter 7

1. Nick Sullivan, "The New State of Small Business," *Home Office Computing*, May 1995, 47.
2. Ibid.
3. Robert L. Rose, "A Foot in the Door," *Wall Street Journal*, 27 February 1985, R7.

Chapter 10

1 Jerry W. Gustafson, "Liberal Education and Work: A Personal View," *Journal of Career Planning and Employment*, Winter 1995, 63.
2. Leonhardt, "Ivy-Colored Halls," ENT18.
3. Anne Murphy, "Do-it-Yourself Job Creation," *Inc.*, January 1994, 38.

4. Donald J. McNerney, "A New Look at Entrepreneurism," *HR Focus*, August 1994, 4.

5. E. Gordon Gee, interview, "Open Line with Fred Andrle," Radio Station WOSU-AM, 30 May 1995, 2:30 P.M.

6. Anthony Robbins, *Unlimited Power* (New York: Ballantine Books, 1986), 200-201.

7. William D. Danko and Thomas J. Stanley, *The Millionaire Next Door* (Atlanta: Longstreet Press, 1996), 9.

Conclusion

1. Cooperative Institutional Research Program, University of California, Los Angeles, "Executive Summary, 2000 CIRP Freshman Survey," 8.

2. Bruce Tulgan and Carolyn A. Martin, Ph.D., "Managing Generation Y" (book excerpt), *Business Week,* 28 September 2001.